Trotskyism

Concepts in Social Thought

Series Editor: Frank Parkin

Published Titles

Concepts in Social Thought

Trotskyism

Alex Callinicos

University of Minnesota Press

Minneapolis

Published by the University of Minnesota Press
2037 University Avenue Southeast, Minneapolis MN 55414.

Printed in Great Britain

Library of Congress Cataloging-in-Publication Data

Callinicos, Alex.
    Trotskyism/Alex Callinicos.
        p. cm – (Concepts in social thought)
    Includes bibliographical references and index.
    ISBN 0–8166–1904–2: $29.95. – ISBN 0–8166–1905–0 (pbk.): $11.95
    1. Trotsky, Leon, 1879–1940.   2. Communism – Soviet Union
– History – 20th century.   3. Communism – History – 20th century.
I. Title.   II. Series.
HX313.8.T76C35   1990
335.43'3 – dc20

The University of Minnesota
is an equal-opportunity
educator and employer.

Contents

Preface and Acknowledgements

As the manuscript of this book was readied for publication in the autumn and winter of 1989, a succession of regimes installed in power in Eastern Europe by Stalin's armies at the end of the Second World War began to collapse under the pressure of popular revolt. This episode, surely one of the most dramatic and moving developments of the century, suggests that the decline of Stalinism as a political and economic system is irreversible. It is, therefore, an appropriate moment to reconsider the socialist tradition founded by Leon Trotsky, which since its inception in 1923 has defined itself in opposition to Stalinism. In writing this book I have accumulated various debts. I am in the first place grateful to Frank Parkin, the editor of the series in which this book appears, and to Ray Cunningham at the Open University Press. My understanding of Trotsky's thought and of the various traditions to which it has given rise owes a great deal to Duncan Hallas's writings; my discussions over the years with Chris Bambery have also been very helpful. Both read and commented on the manuscript, as did Tony Cliff and Chris Harman. I thank them all for their often searching criticisms, even though I have not always followed their advice. While working on this book, I was fortunate enough to meet in Moscow Nadezhda Joffe, daughter of one of the leaders of the Left Opposition and a survivor of Stalin's Gulags. I would like, therefore, to dedicate this book to the memory of those Left Oppositionists who perished in the labour camps, fighting, like the participants in the strike at Vorkuta in 1936–7, for a socialism very different from the regimes currently disintegrating in the East.

List of Abbreviations

CCP	Chinese Communist Party
Comintern	Communist International
FI	Fourth International
IC	International Committee (of the Fourth International)
ICL	International Communist League
IS	International Secretariat (of the Fourth International)
ISC	Independent Socialist Clubs (USA)
ISL	Independent Socialist League (USA)
LCR	Ligue Communiste Révolutionnaire (France)
NEP	New Economic Policy
NLR	*New Left Review*
OCI	Organisation Communiste Internationaliste (France)
PCI	Parti Communiste Internationaliste (France)
RCP	Revolutionary Communist Party (Britain)
RSDLP	Russian Social Democratic Labour Party
SLL	Socialist Labour League (Britain)
SWP	Socialist Workers' Party (Britain, USA)
USFI	United Secretariat of the Fourth International
WIL	Workers' International League (Britain)
WP	Workers' Party (USA)
WRP	Workers' Revolutionary Party (Britain)

Introduction

While Trotskyism has not had a good press among Western social scientists, Leon Trotsky himself is too great a figure to ignore. After his role as one of the chief leaders of the Russian Revolution – President of the St Petersburg Soviet in both 1905 and 1917, organizer of the October rising which brought the Bolsheviks to power, founder of the Red Army, and architect of victory during the Civil War of 1918–21 – Trotsky's subsequent fate – exclusion from power by Stalin and his allies after Lenin's death in 1924, exile from the Soviet Union in 1929, and assassination by an agent of what is now called the KGB in 1940 – lent a tragic quality to a career so intimately involved with the decisive event of the twentieth century. Trotsky's formidable intellectual powers as social theorist, political analyst, and writer – perhaps best displayed in the great *History of the Russian Revolution* (Trotsky 1967) – commanded the respect of many wholly unsympathetic to his politics. Moreover, it was his good fortune to have his life recorded by Isaac Deutscher (1970a; 1970b; 1970c) in what is without doubt one of the outstanding biographies of our time. It is an indication of Trotsky's stature that now, fifty years after his murder, one of the main issues in the reappraisal of the past currently under way in the USSR is the demand for an honest appreciation of his role in the Revolution and its aftermath.

But Trotskyism – the intellectual and political tradition founded by Trotsky – is quite a different matter. One of his lesser biographers, Ronald Segal (1979: 403), dismisses Trotskyism as 'a factional disorder'. This accurately summarizes the dominant image of Trotskyism as a welter of squabbling sects united as much by their complete irrelevance to the realities of political life as by their endless competition for the mantle of orthodoxy inherited from the prophet. As we shall see, this image has a large degree of truth. Yet the marginality and fragmentation of the Trotskyist movement do not of themselves constitute grounds for dismissing the ideas which it embodies and has sought, in various ways, to develop.

Trotskyism as a political current defined itself by the rejection of the two dominant definitions of socialism – those provided by Stalinism in the East and by social democracy in the West – and by the reassertion of what it took to be the traditions of October 1917 – of the revolutionary transformation of society by the proletariat democratically organized through workers' councils. The radical-ism of these ideas helped condemn the Trotskyists to the margins of the labour movement, but the political vision they conjured up attracted in the early years talents as diverse and remarkable as those of the working-class agitator James P. Cannon, the pioneering black writer C. L. R. James, and the Surrealist poet André Breton. In the 1930s and 1940s an astonishingly large number of what later become known as the New York Intellec-tuals became directly or peripherally involved in the American Trotskyist movement – among them Saul Bellow, James Burnham, James T. Farrell, Clement Greenberg, Sidney Hook, Irving Howe, Seymour Martin Lipset, Mary McCarthy, and Dwight Macdonald – before drifting rightwards towards Cold War liberalism or neo-conservatism (see Wald 1987). Revived by the commotions of 1968 and after, many Trotskyist groups were able to attract a new generation of activists. Many of the most important contemporary Marxist theorists can be seen as working in, or from, one variant or other of the Trotskyist tradition – among them, Neville Alexander, Perry Anderson, Daniel Ben-said, Robin Blackburn, Robert Brenner, Pierre Broué, Tony Cliff, Hal Draper, Terry Eagleton, Norman Geras, Adolfo Gilly, Duncan Hallas, Chris Harman, Nigel Harris, Michael Löwy, and Ernest Mandel.

This tradition is best understood as the attempt to continue classical Marxism in conditions defined by, on the one hand, the success of the advanced capitalist countries in weathering revolutionary pressures that were at their greatest in the inter-war years, and, on the other, the betrayal of the hopes raised by the October Revolution by the rise of Stalinism in the USSR and its extension after 1945 to Eastern Europe and China. Deutscher (1984: 245) lamented the

> striking, and to a Marxist often humiliating contrast between what I call classical Marxism – that is, the body of thought developed by Marx, Engels, their contemporaries and after them by Kautsky, Plekhanov, Lenin, Trotsky, Rosa Luxemburg – and the vulgar Marxism, the pseudo-Marxism of the different varieties of European social-democrats, reformists, Stalinists, Krushchevites, and their like.

Anderson (1976) took up the concept of classical Marxism and argued that those coming within its compass were distinguished by their organic involvement in the working-class movement of their day and by a theoretical concentration on the evolution of the capitalist economy, the political forms of bourgeois rule, and the strategy and tactics of class struggle. He contrasted this tradition with that of Western Marxism as it crystallized after the Second World War, a collection of thinkers – among them Adorno, Althusser, Della Volpe, Horkheimer, Marcuse, and Sartre – characterized by their distance from any form of political practice and by their preoccupation with questions of philosophy and aesthetics. Trotskyism, basing itself as it does on the thought of one of the main practitioners of classical Marxism, has generally been intellectually resistant to the themes and vocabulary of Western Marxism. This may help explain the comparative lack of interest in Trotskyism displayed by contemporary social theory, which has, on the whole, been remarkably receptive to Western Marxism. Versions of Marxism formulated within the academy are likely to be more palatable to social scientists than those which still aspire to address the concerns and influence the actions of ordinary working people.

Russell Jacoby's (1987: 5) stimulating polemical essay *The Last Intellectuals* mourns the passing in the United States of 'public intellectuals, writers and thinkers who address a general and educated audience'. The New York Intellectuals represented a passing generation that has not been replaced; the left intelligentsia produced by the movements of the 1960s ended up in the universities where it produces a hermetic academic discourse incomprehensible to outsiders. This change is undeniable, and is not confined to the USA. Jacoby adduces various social causes –

suburbanization, gentrification, the expansion of higher education – which destroyed the milieu in which the old politically engaged intelligentsia flourished and provided a different, and more isolated environment for their successors. No doubt these factors are of great importance, but there is also a political condition which Jacoby ignores. The major political experience shared by many New York Intellectuals was their involvement in the Trotskyist movement, which sought systematically to relate rigorous theoretical enquiry to practical involvement in the public world. Habits acquired in this context stayed with the New York Intellectuals even after they had moved on to very different political commitments. By contrast, the generation of 1960s left intellectuals tended to encounter forms of Marxism – Western Marxism or often highly Stalinist variants of Maoism – which made it much more difficult to combine critical theory and political practice.

Alasdair MacIntyre, himself a sometime Trotskyist, has recently stressed the importance of what he calls 'tradition-constituted enquiry', where

> the standards of rational justification themselves emerge from and are part of a history in which they are vindicated by the way in which they transcend the limitations of and provide remedies for the defects of their predecessors within the history of that same tradition (1988: 7).

One does not have to accept MacIntyre's claim that all criteria of rationality are specific to a particular tradition, let alone the tradition for which he now opts – Augustinian Christianity – to recognize the importance of tracing the manner in which traditions evolve through attempting to resolve the problems internal to them. We shall see that the subsequent history of Trotskyism was shaped by the great crisis of the 1940s, precipitated by the refutation of Trotsky's predictions about the Second World War and its outcome. The differing responses made to this crisis irrevocably shattered the unity of the Trotskyist movement and produced three main theoretico-political strands, radically different from one another but all deriving from Trotsky: the 'orthodox Trotskyism' of the various Fourth Internationals; those revisions of orthodoxy which tended to imply a break with classical Marxism (Shachtman and Castoriadis, for example); and the International

Socialist tradition founded by Cliff, whose critique of orthodox Trotskyism was conceived rather as a *return* to classical Marxism.

It is this process of theoretical development, defined by the divergent solutions offered to the crisis of the 1940s, which forms the subject of the present book. What follows is very far from being a history of the Trotskyist movement – the nature of the series in which this book appears as well as the limitations of my own knowledge dictate this (though I have benefited from the recent explosion of historical research into Trotskyism reflected in the emergence of journals such as *Cahiers Léon Trotsky* and *Revolutionary History*). The aim of this study is rather to provide an intellectual history of Trotskyism as a political movement. The particular examples given are intended primarily to illustrate theoretical issues. These illustrations reflect the bias of my knowledge towards British and American Trotskyism. This has the disadvantage that, for example, the Trotskyist movement in Latin America is completely ignored, despite the fact that some of the most significant organizations are to be found in this region. The study's bias does, nevertheless, have the virtue of bringing out the fact that Trotskyism has enjoyed some of its greatest influence (comparatively) in societies – Britain and the United States – where the general impact of Marxism has been slight. If the history I offer is somewhat stylized – some might say caricatured – it may still serve to dramatize the importance of the issues so fiercely disputed by those who have sought to continue Trotsky's thought.

1
Origins

1.1 Permanent revolution

The origins of what would be later called Trotskyism can be traced back to the event which established Trotsky in the first rank of Russian socialists, the 1905 Revolution. Until that upheaval, which at its climax in the winter of 1905–6 swept him at the age of twenty-six into the leadership of the St Petersburg Soviet of Workers' Deputies, Trotsky had shared in the consensus among Russian Marxists about the immediate political future. Marxism had emerged in Russia at the beginning of the 1880s in reaction to the dominant revolutionary tradition among the intelligentsia, populism. For the populists, deeply influenced by Western socialism, the transformation of Russian society, feudal, predominantly rural, presided over by the absolute monarchy of the tsars, into an industrialized capitalist country like Britain was a disaster to be avoided at all costs. The communal forms of social organization surviving among the peasantry would allow Russia to sidestep the travails of capitalism and move directly to socialism. Increasingly the populists saw their role as that of giving history a push, as Zhelyabov, leader of the terrorist Narodnaya Volya, put it, by physically destroying the autocracy which stood in the way of the socialist future. Plekhanov, the founder of Russian Marxism, set his face against such voluntarism. Socialism, he argued, presupposed a development of the productive forces which only capitalism could achieve. The expansion of the market and consequent disintegration of peasant communities which Lenin in particular analysed and documented at the turn of the century were historically necessary preconditions of socialist revolution.

Russian Marxists on the eve of 1905 were unanimous in recognizing what seemed to be the political corollary of this argument, namely that the coming revolution would be 'bourgeois-democratic'. Like the English and French Revolutions before it, in sweeping away absolutism it would create the political framework within which capitalism could develop unfettered. There were, however, important differences about the role the key social classes would play in Russia's bourgeois revolution. Indeed, the historic split at the 1903 Congress of the Russian Social Democratic Labour Party (RSDLP) between Bolsheviks and Mensheviks, though precipitated by questions of party organization, was consolidated by disagreements over this issue. Plekhanov and the Mensheviks expected the liberal bourgeoisie to play the sort of leading role they believed its English and French counterparts had performed in their revolutions; on this prognosis, the task of the infant Russian workers' movement would be to support the liberals against the tsar – *their* time would come only after the autocracy had been overthrown and capitalism considerably expanded. By contrast, Lenin and the Bolsheviks contended that the belated development of Russian capitalism had rendered the bourgeoisie economically dependent on and politically subordinate to the state and foreign capital: far from leading mass action against the absolutist state the liberals would look to it for protection against a proletariat that was already showing signs of getting out of hand. The workers' movement should in these circumstances assume the role abandoned by the supine bourgeoisie and lead the peasant masses against the tsar. If the RSDLP seized the initiative at a time of popular turmoil, it might succeed in replacing the autocracy with a 'revolutionary-democratic dictatorship of the proletariat and peasantry' which would seek, within the limits of capitalism, to promote conditions as favourable as possible for socialist transformation.

Lenin's analysis proved more accurate than Plekhanov's in both 1905 and 1917: liberal capitalists on both occasions were more afraid of insurgent workers and peasants than of the *ancien régime*. Trotsky, while agreeing with Lenin, went much further. In the first place, he set the development of capitalism in Russia in the context of the world economy. The rapid industrialization promoted by the monarchy in co-operation with foreign capital at the end of the nineteenth century was a response to competitive pressures transmitted through the European state system: military power now required an advanced industrial base. The result was an illustration of what Trotsky (1967: I, 23) would later call 'the law of combined development', the 'drawing together of the different stages of the journey, a combining of separate steps, an amalgam of archaic and more contemporary forms'. By virtue of 'the privilege of historical backwardness', Russia, rather than pass through all the separate stages travelled by countries such as Britain and France on their road to capitalism, could take advantage of the most advanced forms of technology and organization available in the West, importing the latest industrial plant. By the turn of the century, there were some of the largest and most modern factories in the world in Russia, amid vast pools of rural poverty. The new proletariat, concentrated in a few major urban centres, could exert an influence quite out of proportion to its size. Suffering all the social miseries typical of rapid industrialization, denied the most elementary political rights, this working class would, Trotsky (like Lenin) believed play the central role in the struggle against tsarism.

Thereafter the two parted company. The Bolsheviks, Trotsky argued, overestimated the capacity of the peasantry to act as an independent social and political force:

> Because of its dispersion, political backwardness, and especially of its deep inner contradictions which cannot be resolved within the framework of the capitalist system, the peasantry can only deal the old order some powerful blows from the rear, by spontaneous risings in the countryside, on the one hand, and by creating discontent in the army, on the other.
>
> (Trotsky 1973a: 237)

It could only act as a national force under the leadership of an urban class. The peasant parties such as the Social Revolutionaries which Lenin envisaged participating in the 'revolutionary-democratic dictatorship' represented the hegemony of the urban bourgeoisie and petty bourgeoisie over the rural masses. A coalition between such parties and Russian social democracy would inevitably succumb to the contradictions it contained. Either the proletariat would adopt a 'self-denying ordinance', and refuse to use its political power to further its economic interests, in which case its position would be gradually eroded by the bourgeoisie, or it would make inroads into the economic power of capital, for example, by taking over firms which laid off workers, in which case it would have crossed the boundaries of the bourgeois-democratic revolution and established the dictatorship of the proletariat. Trotsky argued that Russian socialists should opt for the second course. Only thus, through a 'permanent revolution' in which bourgeois and socialist elements fused, could tsarism be destroyed.

This position left Trotsky isolated till the outbreak of the Russian Revolution of February 1917. Then the dilemma he had outlined more than a decade previously came to life. The liberal Provisional Government could only survive with the support of the soviets, which it obtained not merely from the Mensheviks and Social Revolutionaries but also from many Bolshevik leaders, including Stalin and Kamenev. Lenin, on his return to Russia in April 1917, rapidly won the party to a very different strategy, the seizure of power by the soviets on the basis of a programme which sanctioned peasant takeovers of the gentry's estates alongside other demands – for example, workers' control of the factories – which implied a commitment to the construction of socialism. As many 'Old Bolsheviks' complained, Lenin's April theses were tantamount to 'Trotskyism'. The Bolsheviks' effective acceptance of the theory of permanent revolution helps explain Trotsky's decision to join the party in the summer of 1917. Another factor was also at work. He had since the 1903 Congress strenuously opposed Lenin's efforts to build a centralized revolutionary party. Like Rosa Luxemburg, Trotsky had believed that the development of mass workers' struggles would generate the transformations of consciousness required for the proletariat to play the independent political role implied by the theory of permanent revolution. The revolutionary party would be primarily a reflection of the evolution of proletarian class consciousness. The February Revolution and its aftermath seem, however, to have convinced Trotsky that Lenin was right: only a politically homogeneous vanguard organization such as the Bolsheviks could give the spontaneous movements of the class struggle the necessary focus upon the conquest of state power. 'Without a guiding organization the energy of the masses would dissipate like steam in a piston-box. But nevertheless what moves things is not the piston or the box, but the steam' (Trotsky 1967: I, 17). From this perspective, without the Bolsheviks the theory of permanent revolution would have remained, despite all Trotsky's gifts as a mass leader, a purely intellectual construction lacking the mechanism capable of putting it into practice.

The Revolution of October 1917, in confirming Trotsky's prognosis, burst asunder the traditional categories of 'orthodox' Marxism. It was, as Gramsci (1977: 34–7) put it, a veritable 'revolution against *Capital*' – in other words, it challenged the schema drawn up by Kautsky, Plekhanov, and other theoreticians of the Second International of history as a series of modes of production succeeding one another by iron necessity and culminating in the inevitable triumph of socialism. It was, however, only a decade later that Trotsky generalized what had been a specific analysis of the peculiarities of Russian historical development into a universal theory of revolution in the backward countries. The occasion was the Chinese Revolution of 1925–7. Stalin and Bukharin, then the leaders of the dominant faction within the Bolsheviks and therefore also in the Third (or Communist) International (Comintern), insisted that the Chinese Communist Party (CCP) adopt a variant of the old Menshevik strategy, participating in a 'four-class bloc' with the nationalist wing of the bourgeoisie, represented by the Guomindang, in order to achieve the 'national-democratic revolution' required to rid China of foreign exploiters. Trotsky backed up a withering critique of the tactical errors involved – the Guomindang, after using the Communists to defeat the warlords, then turned on and massacred them – with the general thesis that the bourgeoisie in the backward countries was no longer capable of playing a revolutionary role. But the same global processes of capitalist development, the interlacing of advanced and backward which Trotsky called uneven and combined development, which bound these capitalists to imperialism, also created in countries such as China and India working classes capable, like their Russian counterpart, of exerting an influence out of proportion to their minority status. The hold of imperialism on the rest of the world could be broken only if the proletariat of the backward countries could lead the mass of peasants in revolutions which both eliminated pre-capitalist and colonial exploitation and initiated the transition to socialism.

In its general form, the theory of permanent revolution implied a direct challenge to what after 1945 became the orthodoxy in Third World national liberation movements influenced by Marxism-Leninism in its Russian, Chinese, or Cuban variants. Whereas these sought to construct coalitions (following the Chinese formula) of workers, peasants, intellectuals, and the 'national bourgeoisie' (that is, those capitalists supposed to have an interest in breaking with imperialism) united by the objective of national independence, Trotsky stressed the class antagonisms within such alliances, and the distinctive character of the proletariat as the only force with both an interest in, and the capacity to achieve, national liberation. A similar theme informs his writings on Europe in the 1930s. Trotsky was fiercely critical of the Comintern's 'third period' policy in the late 1920s and early 1930s, which involved the powerful German Communist Party opposing united action with the Social Democrats against the Nazis on the grounds that one was as bad as the other. He was nevertheless equally opposed to the strategy adopted by Stalin in 1935 of constructing anti-fascist 'Popular Fronts' of the labour movement and the 'democratic' wing of the bourgeoisie. Rather than uniting the working class against fascism, Trotsky argued, the Popular Front governments in France and Spain represented the subordination of proletarian interests to those of capital, with results that could only strengthen Hitler, Mussolini, and Franco. As in the theory of permanent revolution proper, Trotsky here accorded primacy to independent working-class action.

1.2 The critique of Stalinism

The generalization of the theory of permanent revolution made explicit what had earlier been implicit, namely that Trotsky's frame of reference was the capitalist world-system as a whole:

> Marxism takes its starting point from world economy, not as a sum of national parts but as a mighty and independent reality which has been created by the international division of labour and the world market and which in our epoch imperiously dominates the national markets.
>
> (Trotsky 1969: 146)

Accordingly, he argued that while socialist revolution would begin in an individual country it could only be completed on a world scale. The internationalization of the productive forces achieved by capitalism meant that socialism could not be built in one country, and certainly not backward Russia. A workers' state should act primarily as a platform from which to spread the revolution to other countries.

> The socialist revolution begins on the national arena, in unfolds on the international arena, and is completed on the world arena. Thus, the socialist revolution becomes a permanent revolution in a newer and

broader sense; it attains completion only in the final victory of the
new society on the entire planet.

(Trotsky 1969: 279)

In thus rejecting the possibility of socialism in one country, Trotsky
was merely stating what was axiomatic to all Marxists in 1917. Lenin
stressed on numerous occasions that the survival of the Bolshevik
regime depended on the victory of revolutions in the advanced
countries, especially Germany. The Bolsheviks accordingly
launched the Comintern in 1919, with the aim of establishing an
'international Soviet republic'. Marx had indeed warned that
without world revolution 'privation, *want* is merely made general
and with *want* the struggle for necessities would begin again and the
whole filthy business would necessarily be restored' (Marx and
Engels 1976a: 49). This prediction seemed to be confirmed by
developments after 1917. No successful revolution in the West came
to the aid of the Bolshevik regime. Industry collapsed under the
impact of invasion, civil war, and blockade. The urban working
class which had made the Revolution sharply diminished in size and
political enthusiasm. The soviets consequently became the empty
shells of proletarian rule, so that by the end of the Civil War in 1921
the Bolshevik Party, itself transformed into a bureaucratic organization interwoven with the state apparatus, found itself ruling, in the
name of a class which had effectively ceased to exist, over a
population largely made up of small-holding peasants whose
natural suspicions of government were reinforced by the regime's
commitment to collective rather than private ownership.

It was against this background that, in the years after Lenin's
death in January 1924, a bitter factional struggle developed among
the Bolsheviks. Stalin, allied first to Zinoviev and Kamenev and
then to Bukharin, owed his rise to the new bureaucracy of party
secretaries over which he presided. The doctrine of 'socialism in one
country', though formulated by Bukharin, is perhaps best seen as an
assertion of this group's self-confidence. Dismissing the possibilities
of revolutions elsewhere from their calculations, especially after the
German Communist Party's failure to take advantage of the
radicalization produced by the 1923 inflation, Stalin and his
supporters asserted their capacity to reconstruct society using
resources available within Russia's borders. For much of the 1920s
the strategy formulated by Bukharin and the Right of the party was

accepted as the best means of achieving this objective. This involved extending the New Economic Policy (NEP) introduced at the end of the Civil War to conciliate the peasantry by relying on market incentives rather than coercion to provide the towns with food, even if this meant industry growing 'at a snail's pace', as Bukharin put it. Trotsky and the Left Opposition rejected this policy because it was likely to promote the development of rural petty capitalism which would provide the socio-economic base for counter-revolution. Faster industrial growth would increase the size and social weight of the working class, a necessary condition of the restoration of democracy in both party and soviets. Nevertheless, Trotsky argued, no purely national strategy could resolve the contradictions facing the Bolshevik regime. Thus a major theme of the Left's critique of Stalin and Bukharin was the manner in which socialism in one country led to the subordination of the Comintern to the interests of Russian foreign policy and therefore to the squandering of major revolutionary opportunities – for example, in China in 1925–7 and in Britain during the General Strike of 1926.

The final defeat of the Opposition in 1927–8 – which recent research has shown to have been less of a foregone conclusion than previously thought – took place in the context of an increasingly serious crisis involving worsening relations with the West, industrial stagnation, and an abrupt fall in grain deliveries (Reiman 1987). Stalin's response was to break with the Right and resort to coercion to extract from the peasants the grain needed to feed the cities. This expedient became the starting point for a different strategy involving rapid centrally directed industrialization and the forced collectivization of agriculture. Implemented during the First Five Year Plan (1928–32), the new policy transformed the USSR into a major industrial power, but at an enormous human price: collectivization led to the deaths of millions of peasants from repression, famine, or forced labour in the Gulag Archipelago. Even modern Soviet estimates suggest that industrialization was financed by a drastic reduction in real wages. The divisions these consequences caused inside the regime led in 1936 to the Great Purge in which much of the old Bolshevik Party perished.

Exiled from the USSR in January 1929, Trotsky sought to provide a Marxist explanation of this enormous transformation. Given its unprecedented character, it is hardly surprising that his views on the subject should have undergone considerable changes.

The thread running through these modifications is a preoccupation with the social causes of Stalinism. As early as December 1923 Trotsky (1975: 91) was insisting that '[b]ureacratism is a social phenomenon'. Stalin was the representative of a distinct social layer, the bureaucratic 'caste' which had crystallized within the party and state after 1917. It was not, however, from the bureaucracy that Trotsky expected a Russian equivalent of 9 Thermidor (27 July 1794), when the Jacobin dictatorship under Robespierre was overthrown and a conservative reaction unleashed. The main danger of counter-revolution came, rather, from the 'new bourgeoisie' of *kulaks* (rich peasants) and nepmen (speculators and middlemen) who had benefited from the revival of the private market under NEP. The Stalinist bureaucracy Trotsky saw as a 'centrist' force: just as left social democrats such as Kautsky vacillated between reform and revolution, so Stalin balanced between the two main classes – the 'new bourgeoisie' represented by Bukharin and the Right and the proletariat championed by Trotsky and the Left. Hence Stalin's zigzag from an alliance with Bukharin in the mid-1920s to forced industrialization and collectivization in 1928, a shift which many supporters of the Left Opposition welcomed as the adoption of their own policy, even though Trotsky himself had advocated much lower growth targets than those set in the First Five Year Plan and opposed the coercion of the peasantry into collective farms.

The events of 1927–8 did not lead Trotsky to alter his basic appraisal of the regime. He rejected the argument, advanced by Viktor Smirnov and the Democratic Centralist faction as early as 1926, that a counter-revolution had occurred (see Ciliga 1979: 261–91 on the debates within the Left Opposition). Thermidor, in the sense of 'the restoration of capitalism', remained a 'danger' rather than accomplished reality (Trotsky 1981:321–3). Russia was still a workers' state, despite the bureaucratization of party and soviets. 'The zig-zags of Stalinism show that the bureaucracy is not a class, not an independent historical factor, but an instrument, an executive organ of the classes' (Trotsky 1973b: 215). The Stalinist regime represented a form of Bonapartism: like the Second Empire of Napoleon III (as analysed by Marx in *The Eighteenth Brumaire of Louis Bonaparte*), its power arose from an equilibrium between bourgeoisie and proletariat rather than from an independent socio-economic base. The task of the Left Opposition was not forcibly to overthrow the bureaucracy in a second revolution but to subject it to democratic control by peaceful means:

> As the situation is now, the bourgeoisie could seize power only by *the road of counterrevolutionary upheaval*. As for the proletariat, it can regain full power, overhaul the bureaucracy, and put it under its control by *the road of reform of the party and the soviets*.
>
> (Trotsky 1981: 295)

It was not any change within the USSR but the failure of the Comintern's strongest section outside Russia to prevent the Nazi seizure of power in Germany which led Trotsky to change this assessment. 'Now we are in a new historic stage in which the policy of reform is exhausted', he declared in July 1933 (Trotsky 1972b: 27). Furthermore, '[t]he Thermidor of the Great Russian Revolution is not before us, but already far behind', having taken place in 1924 (Trotsky 1971b: 182). The Russian Thermidor did not, however, represent 'the first stage of the bourgeois counter-revolution, aimed against the social basis of the workers' state', as the Left Opposition had argued in the 1920s (Trotsky 1971b: 173). The USSR was still a workers' state, albeit a degenerated one. Presiding over a 'transitional society' between capitalism and socialism, the state had 'a dual character: socialistic, insofar as it defends social property in the means of production; bourgeois, insofar as the distribution of life's goods is carried out with a capitalistic measure of the value and all the consequences ensuing therefrom' (Trotsky 1970:54). This contradiction was intensified by the 'generalized want' arising from Russia's isolation after the Revolution:

> The basis of bureaucratic rule is the poverty of society in objects of consumption, with the resulting struggle of each against all. When there is enough goods in a store, the purchasers can come whenever they want to. When there is little goods, the purchasers are compelled to stand in line. When the lines are very long, it is necessary to appoint a policeman to keep order. Such is the starting point of the power of the Soviet bureaucracy.
>
> (Trotsky 1970: 112)

If the bureaucracy was a product of post-Revolutionary scarcity, it was able thereafter to reshape Soviet society in its own interests, monopolizing political power and claiming for itself a host of material privileges. Trotsky nevertheless insisted that the bureaucracy, though 'the planter and protector of inequality' (Trotsky 1970: 113), was not a new ruling class. He vehemently opposed the claims by some of his supporters that Stalinism represented either state capitalism or a new variant of class society, bureaucratic collectivism. The bureaucracy was 'a temporary growth', 'the product of an "accidental" (i.e., temporary and extraordinary) enmeshing of historical circumstances', above all the failure of revolution in the West (Trotsky 1973c: 6). The relations of production were still those established by the October Revolution:

> The nationalization of the land, the means of industrial production, transport and exchange, together with the monopoly of foreign trade, constitute the basis of the Soviet social structure. Through these relations, established by the proletarian revolution, the nature of the Soviet Union as a proletarian state is for us basically defined.
>
> (Trotsky 1970: 248)

State ownership of the means of production was thus a necessary and sufficient condition of the existence of a workers' state. As Max Shachtman (1962: 92) pointed out, this amounted to the abandonment of the criterion Trotsky had used earlier, 'namely, *Does the working class still have political power, in one sense or another, even if only in the sense that it is still capable of bringing a straying and dangerous bureaucracy under its control by means of reform measures?*'. Trotsky (1970: 288–9) now believed that the working class could only remove the Stalin regime by revolutionary means, but that this would be a 'political revolution', which would leave intact the 'economic foundations' of Soviet society, amounting rather to 'a second supplementary revolution – against bureaucratic absolutism'.

1.3 Revolutionary prospects

The conclusion, however qualified, that a new revolution was required in the USSR, placed a heavy burden on the shoulders of Trotsky and his followers. Although increasingly subject to repression by the secret police within the USSR, the Left Opposition was able to attract a scattering of support in the various Communist parties. Often accident played a role: James P. Cannon, then a leader of the Communist Party of the USA, read a document by

Trotsky which was distributed by mistake to delegates of the Sixth Congress of the Comintern in 1928 and was convinced by the arguments it contained. As was usual in such cases, Cannon was soon expelled from the CPUSA. Nevertheless, the International Communist League (ICL), formed by the Trotskyists in 1930, regarded itself until 1933 as a faction of the Comintern, committed in line with Trotsky's reform perspective to winning the Communist movement away from its Stalinist leadership. Hitler's victory in Germany, however, represented for Trotsky an event comparable to the Second International's capitulation to imperialist war in August 1914, proclaiming the Comintern's irredeemable bankruptcy. It was necessary now to build a new (Fourth) International which, while basing itself on the Bolshevik tradition and on the first four congresses of the Comintern (1919–22), would seek to build revolutionary parties in place of the bankrupt Stalinist organizations.

The task thus set was immense. The ICL enjoyed negligible support. Its two most important sections were probably the Russian and the Chinese (to which many CCP leaders had rallied after the débâcle of 1925–7). The Russian Left Opposition was destroyed in the late 1920s by mass arrests and deportations to the Gulag, where its supporters displayed such courage and determination – notably in the hunger strike they organized at Vorkuta in 1936–7 – as to earn even Solzhenitsyn's (1976: 303–7, 372–6) grudging admiration, though not to save them from execution. The fate of the Chinese Trotskyists was little less tragic – they were broken by the repression mounted against them by the Guomindang, the CCP under Mao Zedong, and the Japanese occupying forces alike (see Wang 1980). The ICL's effective membership was therefore concentrated in Europe and the Americas. Its sections in these countries were tiny – one of the most important, the American Communist League, claimed 154 members in 1931. Worse, the persecution of the Trotskyist movement by the Communist parties – reaching a crescendo during the Moscow trials of 1936–8, which sought to establish that Trotsky, along with other Bolshevik leaders such as Zinoviev, Kamenev, and Bukharin, was in league with Hitler – helped confine these groups to the margins of the working-class movement. While there were exceptions – the American Trotskyists were transformed by their role in leading a mass strike of teamsters in Minneapolis in 1934 (Dobbs 1972), and the first

British group was in large part a continuation of an older tradition of proletarian Marxist autodidacts (Groves 1974; MacIntyre 1980) – the ICL sections typically occupied a social milieu frequently described by Trotsky as 'petty bourgeois', a ghetto of middle-class intellectuals for whom sectarian disputation all too often became an end in itself.

The ICL's chief asset in these circumstances was Trotsky himself. His stature as, with Lenin, the chief leader of the October Revolution earned him international attention out of proportion to his actual political influence. Trotsky's years in exile were enormously productive intellectually. Not only did he write some of his greatest works – *My Life, The History of the Russian Revolution, The Revolution Betrayed* – but in a series of occasional pieces he examined the major crises of the day – the rise of Nazism, the Spanish Civil War, the Popular Front in France – creating a body of political analysis which can only be compared, in its scope and penetration, to such writings of Marx's as *The Eighteenth Brumaire* and *The Civil War in France*. Yet the intellectual power of this body of writing is matched only by its complete lack of political impact. The most striking case is that of the series of articles and pamphlets in which Trotsky (1971a), with prescience and increasing urgency, analysed the social roots and political dynamic of German fascism and warned of the disaster that would follow the failure of the Communists and Social Democrats to unite against Hitler. Among Trotsky's greatest writings, they had no influence on events in Germany, where the ICL section amounted at the time of the Nazi victory to perhaps a hundred members.

Trotsky therefore sought, through a succession of different tactics, both to increase the ICL's size and to root its affiliates in the working-class movement. Perhaps the most important of these stratagems was the 'French turn' – so called because Trotsky first proposed it for the French group in June 1934 – which involved the ICL sections joining the social-democratic parties, which were then experiencing a revival and indeed radicalization largely in response to the destruction of the German and Austrian labour movements in 1933–4. This first use of the tactic of 'entrism' by Trotskyists did not involve any expectation that they could take over and transform the social-democratic parties. Indeed Trotsky (1977: 125) argued that '[e]ntry into a reformist [or] centrist party in itself does not include a long perspective. It is only a stage which under certain conditions can be limited to an episode.' But the French turn did not bring about any qualitative change in the situation of the ICL. In a remarkable interview with C. L. R. James in April 1939, Trotsky (1974: 251–2) acknowledged:

> We are not progressing politically. Yes, it is a fact, which is an expression of a general decay of the workers' movements in the last fifteen years. It is the most general cause. When the revolutionary movement in general is declining, when one defeat follows another, when fascism is spreading over the world, when the official 'Marxism' is the most powerful organization of deception of the workers and so on, it is an inevitable situation that the revolutionary elements must work against the general historic current, even if our ideas, our explanations are as exact and wise as one can demand.

Despite these adverse circumstances, Trotsky decided to press ahead and launch the Fourth International (FI) to replace the Comintern. At its founding conference on 3 September 1938, attended by delegates from eleven sections, the Fourth International (World Party of the Socialist Revolution) – to give the new International its full name – claimed, probably optimistically, 5,395 members, of whom no less than 2,500 belonged to by far the strongest group, the Socialist Workers' Party (SWP) in the United States (Reisner 1973: 288–9).

Trotsky (1974: 87) nevertheless predicted: 'During the next ten years the programme of the Fourth International will become the guide of millions and these revolutionary millions will know how to storm earth and heaven.' What grounds did he have for such optimism?

In the first place, Trotsky had a rather catastrophic assessment of the economic prospects of world capitalism. 'Mankind's productive forces stagnate', he declared in the FI's programme, *The Death Agony of Capitalism and the Tasks of the Fourth International* (Reisner 1973: 180). The likelihood of any sustained recovery from the Great Depression which had struck the global economy after the 1929 Wall Street crash was negligible. Indeed, '[t]he disintegration of capitalism has reached extreme limits . . . The further existence of this system is impossible' (Trotsky 1973c: 8). The only obstacle to its overthrow lay in the domination of the workers' movement by forces – Stalinism and social democracy – which did everything in their power to prevent socialist revolution.

Consequently, '[t]he historical crisis of mankind is reduced to the crisis of the revolutionary leadership' (Reisner 1973: 181). Only the absence of authentic revolutionary parties prevented the conquest of power by the working class. The scale of the economic crisis, however, would provide the means for resolving this crisis of leadership:

> The orientation of the masses is determined first by the objective conditions of decaying capitalism, and second, by the treacherous politics of the old workers' organizations. Of these factors, the first is of course the decisive one: the laws of history are stronger than the bureaucratic apparatus . . . As time goes on, their [the Stalinists' and social democrats'] efforts to hold back the wheel of history will demonstrate more clearly to the masses that the crisis of proletarian leadership . . . can be resolved only by the Fourth International.
> (Reisner 1973: 182)

It is in passages such as this that Trotsky seems most vulnerable to the charge of historical fatalism. The claim is sometimes made that the assumption that the development of the productive forces renders socialist revolution inevitable is constitutive of his thought (Hodgson 1975; Molyneux 1981; Beilharz 1987). This seems much too strong. The experience of the 1917 Revolution, and in particular of the role played by the Bolsheviks led Trotsky (1972a: I, 211) to argue that '[f]aith in automatic evolution is the most important and characteristic trait of opportunism' and to stress (Trotsky 1972a: I, 228) the importance of 'the subjective factors of history – the revolutionary will and the revolutionary consciousness of the working class'. He even argued that without Lenin the Bolsheviks might have failed to seize the opportunity offered by the fall of the tsar (Trotsky 1967: I, 310). But it does seem that, in the atmosphere of isolation, persecution and defeat to which Trotsky and his followers were condemned in the late 1930s, he gave way, at times at least, to the belief that 'the laws of history' would allow the FI to gain a mass following.

Trotsky was also influenced by a historical analogy. In the last few years of his life he frequently compared his present situation with that of the extreme left of the Second International during the First World War. Initially isolated and subjected to repression, Lenin, Rosa Luxemburg, Karl Liebknecht and other revolutionary opponents of the war found they were able to gain increasing sympathy for their stance as discontent grew at the front and in the factories – a process which culminated in the Russian Revolutions of 1917 and the German Revolution of 1918. As it became clear that another world war was inevitable, Trotsky predicted that it, too, would end amid social convulsions. After the outbreak of the Second World War he claimed: 'The war will last until it exhausts all the resources of civilization or until it breaks its head on the revolution' (Trotsky 1973d: 151). The upheavals Trotsky foresaw – and which he expected would be, if anything, greater than those of 1917–18 – would allow the FI, like the Bolsheviks before them, to escape from their isolation and gain the confidence of growing numbers of workers. (He was not alone in this prognosis: in the last days of peace the French ambassador to Berlin told Hitler that 'as a result of the war, there would be only one real victor – Mr Trotsky' (Trotsky 1973d: 122).)

A third consideration underlying Trotsky's hopes for the FI concerned the USSR. In China, Germany, France, and Spain the influence of the Communist parties on the most militant sections of the working class had led to squandered revolutionary opportunities. The Second World War would, however, in all probability doom the Stalin regime to collapse. Trotsky (1973d: 201–2) wrote in May 1940:

> the epoch of great convulsions upon which mankind has entered will strike the Kremlin oligarchy with blow after blow, will break up its totalitarian apparatus, will raise the self-confidence of the working masses and thereby facilitate the formation of the Soviet section of the Fourth International.

His belief that the Stalinist bureaucracy was 'but a special, exceptional and temporary refraction' of 'the general laws of modern society . . . under the conditions of a backward revolutionary country in a capitalist environment' was one of Trotsky's chief reasons for resisting the arguments of Shachtman and his supporters that the USSR was a new, bureaucratic-collectivist, class society (see Section 4.1 below). 'Might we not place ourselves in a ludicrous position', he protested in September 1939, 'if we fixed to the Bonapartist oligarchy the nomenclature of a new ruling class just a few years or even a few months prior to its inglorious downfall?' (Trotsky 1973c: 7, 14).

Trotsky died at the hands of a Russian agent on 21 August 1940.

Within five years events were to demonstrate the flaws in the analysis on which he had based his very optimistic expectations about the growth of the FI. These errors should not, however, be allowed to obscure the scale of Trotsky's achievement during the years of exile. In circumstances of great adversity he sought to preserve the classical Marxist tradition, not merely by reaffirming its principal propositions, but by extending it, first, in the general theory of revolutionary strategy and tactics implicit in his writings on Britain, Germany, China, Spain, and France (see Hallas 1979), and, secondly, in the Marxist explanation of Stalinism which he initiated, above all in *The Revolution Betrayed* (Trotsky 1970). Trotsky ensured the continuity of the revolutionary socialist tradition also through his efforts to build the FI. He confided to his diary in March 1935:

> I cannot speak of the 'indispensability' of my own work, even for the period from 1917 to 1921. But now my work is 'indispensable' in the full sense of the word. There is no arrogance in this claim at all. The collapse of the two Internationals [of social democracy and Stalinism] has posed a problem which none of the leaders of these Internationals is at all equipped to solve. The vicissitudes of my personal fate have confronted me with this problem and armed me with important experience in dealing with it. There is now no one except me to carry out the mission of arming a new generation with the revolutionary method over the heads of the leaders of the Second and Third Internationals . . . I need at least five more years of uninterrupted work to ensure the succession.
>
> (Trotsky 1963: 46–7)

Trotsky had those five years, during which he trained the 'new generation' in the tradition which had triumphed, albeit briefly, in October 1917. But his heirs were all too soon put to the test of confronting a world very different from the one Trotsky's predictions at the end of his life had led them to anticipate.

Crisis

2.1 Refuted conjectures

The Trotskyist movement greeted the Second World War as a continuation of the First, an inter-imperialist conflict springing from competition for control over the world's resources between the Great Powers (Trotsky 1973d: 183–222; Mandel 1986). In line, therefore, with the general approach developed by Lenin during the Great War, the FI refused to side with the Western Allies against the Axis powers: 'The victory of the imperialists of Great Britain and France would be no less frightful for the ultimate fate of mankind than that of Hitler and Mussolini' (Trotsky 1973d: 221). Trotsky sought, however, to take account of the general support given the war by the Western labour movement as a struggle against fascism through what came to be known as the Proletarian Military Policy, according to which the FI in the liberal democracies should make the focus of its agitation less outright opposition to the war than demands, based on the claim that the ruling class lacked the will or ability to fight fascism, for trade-union control of the military training of workers and the democratization of the armed forces (Bambery 1989). Ably defended by Cannon (1970) in the 1941 trial of SWP leaders for sedition, the policy was applied with relative success in Britain, where the Workers' International League (WIL) was able to take advantage of the Communist Party's opposition to strikes after the German invasion of the USSR and give expression to some of the industrial discontent which developed in the latter part of the war (Bornstein and Richardson 1986b: chs 1, 3, 5). On the continent of Europe, the Trotskyists had to grapple with much starker questions – that of survival under the German occupation and of the relationship between their own activities and those of the Resistance movements, often led by Communists and informed by patriotic sentiments at odds with the FI's revolutionary internationalism. With extraordinary courage and in extremely adverse circumstances, Trotskyists conducted their own distinctive agitation – in France, for example, producing a paper aimed at disaffected members of the occupying forces, and often paying, as in this case, the price of arrest, torture and execution (Prager 1988).

The German occupation further strengthened the position within the FI of the American SWP, already before the war the largest section, furthermore enjoying a close relationship with Trotsky in his final Mexican exile. Cannon had been profoundly influenced by the factional conflict which broke out in August 1939 and culminated in the departure in April 1940 of Shachtman with some 40 per cent of the membership to form the breakaway Workers' Party (WP). Shachtman argued, with the support of other SWP leaders such as Martin Abern and James Burnham, that events such as the Hitler–Stalin pact confirmed that the Soviet Union was no longer a workers' state and that therefore the FI could no longer unconditionally defend the USSR in war. Although Trotsky reaffirmed his analysis of the USSR as a degenerated workers' state, of which defence of the Soviet Union was a corollary, much of the debate focused on the Shachtmanites' claim that the Cannon leadership represented 'the tendency of bureaucratic conservatism' (Shachtman 1940: 51). Trotsky and Cannon responded by denouncing them as a 'petty bourgeois opposition' which had capitulated to pressures from the liberal intelligentsia (Trotsky 1973c: 43ff.). Burnham and Shachtman (1939: 20) had themselves analysed the process through which many American intellectuals, attracted to left-wing politics and even Trotskyism under the impact of the Depression and the victories of European fascism, in the late 1930s drifted towards 'Stalinophobia, or vulgar anti-Stalinism', and the acceptance of Western capitalist democracy. The subsequent history of most of the Shachtmanites suggests that they were indeed an instance of this phenomenon (see Section 4.1 below). One consequence of the 1940 split was, however, to encourage Cannon to place an exaggerated emphasis on the virtues of orthodoxy and to treat criticism as a reflection of 'the pressure of class forces upon the proletarian vanguard' (Cannon 1972: 1).

These attitudes informed the SWP's approach to reconstituting the FI as an effective organization in the latter years of the war. The Cannon leadership had come into conflict with Jean Van Heijenoort, the secretary of the FI, who, together with a minority faction inside the SWP led by Albert Goldman and Felix Morrow, argued against the majority's insistence that there could be no restoration of bourgeois democracy at the end of the war (see, for example, Morrow 1944; Frank 1944). The SWP leadership used the first post-war gathering of the FI, the International Conference of April 1946, to establish a new International Secretariat (IS). Although its principal figures, notably the Greek Michael Raptis and the Belgian Ernest Mandel – better known by the pseudonyms of Pablo and Germain, respectively – had first emerged in the Trotskyist Resistance and served on the Provisional European Secretariat secretly established in the summer of 1943, they owed their new prominence primarily to American patronage. As Cannon (1973a: 73) later put it,

> Our relations with the leadership in Europe at that time were relations of the closest collaboration and support. There was general agreement between us. These were unknown men in our party. Nobody had ever heard of them. We helped to publicize the individual leaders . . . They had yet to gain authority, not only here but throughout the world. And the fact that the SWP supported them up and down the line greatly reinforced their position.

The situation confronting the 'unknown men' and their backers was one that apparently confounded Trotsky's predictions of a post-war revolutionary wave. Europe was indeed swept during the latter part of the war by a popular radicalization which found its main expression in the Resistance movements in occupied Europe and in the election of the first majority Labour government in Britain. The United States experienced a succession of major strikes which reached their climax in 1945–6. Political agitation was widespread in the American and British armed forces, reflecting discontent which led in some cases to mutiny. But this unrest, while in its scale in accord with Trotsky's prediction of an 'epoch of social convulsion', did not augur revolution. The greatest threat to the Western powers, the Communist-led Resistance movements in France and Italy, was defused thanks to Stalin: in line with his commitments to Roosevelt and Churchill, Communist party leaders such as Thorez and Togliatti instructed their members to disarm and obey the governments installed by the Allies (Claudin, 1975: ch. 5). Further east, the Stalin regime itself, which Trotsky (1973d: 18) had predicted would not outlive the war, emerged, on the contrary, greatly strengthened. Having borne the brunt of the military struggle against Hitler, the USSR rapidly established itself as the dominant power in Eastern Europe through the presence of its armies and the progressive establishment of one-party Communist regimes in Poland, Czechoslovakia and the other Soviet occupied states. The political vitality of Stalinism was further confirmed when in 1949 the CCP, Stalinist in ideology and method despite its differences with Moscow, seized power in China. Far from collapsing, 'the Bonapartist oligarchy' had reproduced itself from the Elbe to the Pacific.

This outcome challenged some of the fundamental assumptions informing the analysis which provided the basis of Trotsky's decision to launch the FI. In the first place, his belief that capitalism was experiencing its final crisis, from which there could be only the most temporary relief, underlay Trotsky's prediction that one of the main casualties of the war would be even the limited bourgeois form of democracy which in countries such as Britain allowed a trade-union movement dominated by reformist politics to flourish:

> All the countries will come out of the war so ruined that the standard of living for the workers will be thrown back a hundred years. Reformist unions are possible only under the regime of bourgeois democracy. But the first to be vanquished in the war will be the thoroughly rotten democracy. In its definitive downfall it will drag with it all the workers' organizations which served as its support.
>
> (Trotsky 1973d: 213)

It was in line with such a catastrophic perspective that Ted Grant could declare in 1943 on behalf of the WIL that Britain was in 'a pre-revolutionary situation' and that the WIL's successor, the Revolutionary Communist Party (RCP), could compare the Attlee government with Kerensky's (Grant 1989: 31, 131). By 1946, the RCP leadership was forced to acknowledge that '*economic activity in Western Europe in the next period is not one of "stagnation and slump" but of revival and boom*' (Grant 1989: 381). They did not dream, however, that the world economy was on the verge of the longest, most sustained boom in its history, which would see world gross national product grow three-and-a-half times between 1948 and 1973.

The survival and expansion of Stalinism posed an even more acute problem for Trotsky's heirs. The Eastern European states experienced after 1945 a process of what Mandel called 'structural assimilation' to the USSR. Particularly after the onset of the Cold War in 1946–7, the Communist monopoly of political power was established and widespread nationalizations carried out. The outcome was socio-economic structures in essentials identical to that of the USSR. Were what the FI liked to call the 'buffer states' themselves workers' states, as Trotsky had claimed Stalinist Russia to be? To answer this question in the negative involved a refusal consistently to apply the criterion of a workers' state which Trotsky himself had given, namely state ownership of the means of production and monopoly of foreign trade (see Section 1.2 above). But to treat the Eastern European regimes as workers' states – though, like the USSR, bureaucratized ones – would have profound consequences for the theoretical structure of Trotskyism and for its very existence as a political movement.

For one thing, the transformations carried out in Eastern Europe after 1945 were 'revolutions from above', in which the decisive role had been played by the Communist parties with the support of the Russian occupying forces. The Red Army had, during its advance westwards in 1944–5, taken care to suppress the various moves made to carry out a social revolution from below, disbanding workers' councils and popular militias. The mass demonstrations accompanying the Prague coup of February 1948 were orchestrated by a Communist Party whose power derived primarily from its control over the army and police and from Russian backing (see Harman 1983: ch. 1). This was a process radically at odds with the conception of socialist revolution formulated by Marx under the inspiration of the Paris Commune of 1871, and reaffirmed by Lenin in *The State and Revolution*, in which the working class would dismantle the existing bureaucratic apparatus of state power, including the standing army and police, and replace it with organs (such as the soviets in the Russian Revolutions of 1905 and 1917) based upon direct popular participation and control. Nor were those Stalinist victories which occurred without Russian military intervention, above all in China and Yugoslavia, any more compatible with this classical Marxist conception of revolution. In these countries the decisive role had been played by Communist-led peasant armies employing a strategy of guerrilla warfare which was to have many imitators in the Third World in the subsequent half-century. But Trotsky, like Marx before him, had always rejected the possibility of the peasantry acting as the agent of socialist revolution. He even envisaged, in the event of a revival of the Chinese workers' movement in the cities under Trotskyist leadership, 'a civil war between the peasant army led by the Stalinists and the proletarian vanguard led by the Leninists' (Trotsky 1976a: 530).

If therefore the Eastern European and Chinese regimes were workers' states, then Marx and Engels (1965: 327) were mistaken when they declared: 'The emancipation of the working class is conquered by the working classes themselves.' Accordingly, Mandel in 1946 described the idea that socialist revolutions had taken place in Eastern Europe as 'a complete petty bourgeois revision of the Marxist-Leninist concept both of the state and of the proletarian revolution' (quoted in Cliff 1982: 83). The vehemence of this reaction reflected a further consideration. Trotsky had argued that the Stalinist bureaucracy, although still resting on the social foundations laid by the October Revolution, was a conservative force whose global role had become that of preventing rather than stimulating revolution: 'The bureaucracy which became a reactionary force in the USSR cannot play a revolutionary role on the world arena' (Reisner 1973: 214). But if Stalinist parties had overturned capitalism in China and Eastern Europe, then the bureaucracy had proved to be a profoundly *revolutionary* force. Furthermore, if Stalinism could in fact make socialist revolutions, then what was the role of the FI, the putative 'World Party of the Socialist Revolution'? Responding to comparisons between the supposed establishment of workers' states in the 'buffer zone' and the bourgeois 'revolution from above' carried out by Bismarck in Germany, the Palestinian Trotskyist and RCP leader Tony Cliff (1982: 66) commented:

> The 'Bismarckian' path was not the exception for the bourgeoisie, but the rule. The exception was the French revolution. If the proletarian revolution can be carried out not necessarily through the activity of the working class itself but by a state bureaucracy, then the Russian revolution would inevitably be the exception while the 'Bismarckian' path would be the rule. The rise of the bourgeoisie was based on the deception of the masses, whether the French sansculottes or the soldiers of Bismarck. If a proletarian revolution can be

carried out without an independent revolutionary leadership there is no reason at all for this leadership to appear. The law of lesser resistance will lead history to choose the path of revolution carried out by small minorities deceiving the big majorities.

The post-war transformation of Eastern Europe by the USSR in its own likeness presented Trotsky's heirs with the following dilemma: to abandon his identification of the overthrow of capitalism with state ownership of the means of production or to revise the classical Marxist conception of socialist revolution as 'the self-conscious, independent movement of the immense majority, in the interest of the immense majority', (Marx and Engels 1976b: 495). 'Orthodox Trotskyism', as Cannon was the first to call it, consisted in taking the second horn of this dilemma.

2.2 Conventionalist stratagems

The crisis of the Trotskyist movement after 1945 is an instance of quite a common problem in the history of the sciences. Imre Lakatos (1978: I) suggested that theories are best seen as 'scientific research programmes' which develop through the formulation of successive refutable auxiliary hypotheses. Where a research programme predicts 'novel facts' it is 'theoretically progressive', and where some of these predictions are empirically corroborated it is 'empirically progressive'. A programme which fails to predict, or whose hypotheses are refuted, is by contrast, 'degenerating', a prime candidate for replacement by another programme, as Copernicus's supplanted Ptolemy's in astronomy or Einstein's Newton's in physics. Each programme has a 'hard core' of hypotheses which are treated as being immune from refutation, unlike the dispensable auxiliary hypotheses. One sign of a degenerating programme is the emergence of what Karl Popper (1970: 82–4) called 'conventionalist stratagems', designed to protect the hard core from the persistent refutation of its auxiliary hypotheses, in the way that Ptolemy's late medieval followers sought to render his geocentric model of the planetary system consistent with observation by tacking on epicycles.

Popper and Lakatos alike defined a scientific theory as one that stipulates the conditions of its own refutation. Interestingly, Trotsky in one of his last writings fulfilled this requirement. During the 1939–40 debate with Shachtman and Burnham he argued that if the Second World War did not lead to a revolution which would settle accounts with Stalinism and capitalism alike,

> it would be necessary in retrospect to establish that in its fundamental traits the present USSR was the precursor of a new exploiting class on an international scale . . . The historic alternative, carried to the end, is as follows: either the Stalin regime is an abhorrent relapse in the process of transforming bourgeois society into a socialist society, or the Stalin regime is the first stage of a new exploiting society. If the second prognosis proves to be correct, then of course, the bureaucracy will become a new exploiting class. However onerous the second perspective may be, if the world proletariat should actually prove incapable of fulfilling the mission placed upon it by the course of development, nothing else would remain except only to recognize that the socialist programme, based on the internal contradictions of capitalist society, ended as a Utopia.
>
> (Trotsky 1973c: 9)

Trotsky thus believed that the refutation of his predictions would place in doubt the truth of Marxism itself. Perhaps in part because the stakes were thereby raised very high, Cannon and his 'unknown men' in the IS initially refused to recognize any conflict between Trotsky's prognoses and the development of world politics at the end of the war. In what is a classic example of a conventionalist stratagem, Cannon (1977: 200) even declared in November 1945:

> Trotsky predicted that the fate of the Soviet Union would be decided in the war. That remains our firm conviction. Only we disagree with some people who carelessly think the war is over. The war has only passed through one stage and is now in the process of regroupment and reorganization for the second. The war is not over, and the revolution which we said would issue from the war in Europe is not taken off the agenda. It has only been delayed and postponed, primarily for lack of a sufficiently strong revolutionary party.

If the facts didn't fit the theory, so much the worse for the facts. Similarly, the International Conference declared in April 1946 that Europe would 'remain on a level approaching stagnation and slump' (quoted in Grant 1989: 380). This claim, and its corollary, that there could be no restoration of bourgeois democracy, was challenged by the French section of the FI, the Parti Communiste Internationaliste (PCI), and the British RCP. On the latter's behalf,

Cliff (1982: 24–39) was able very effectively to refute Mandel's attempts to explain away the abundant evidence of economic recovery. Similarly, Grant (1989: 125) pointed out what was evident to everyone except the IS and the SWP leadership: 'Everywhere in Western Europe since the "liberation", the tendency has been for a steady movement towards bourgeois democracy and not towards greater and greater dictatorial regimes'. Nevertheless, although the RCP leadership displayed a greater sense of reality than Cannon or Mandel, they too believed that the revolution predicted by Trotsky had only been postponed. Thus Grant (1989: 381) argued that a 'new recovery can only prepare the way for an even greater slump and economic crisis than in the past'.

The nature of the 'buffer zone' in Eastern Europe was, however, the greatest source of difficulty. The initial reaction of the FI leadership was to refuse to regard Moscow's new satellites as workers' states. Mandel argued on behalf of the IS in September 1946: 'The nature of the economy and of the state remains bourgeois in these countries' (quoted in Frank 1969: 48). This position, though reaffirmed at the Second Congress of the FI in April 1948 (Fourth International 1948), was too evidently in conflict with the identity of social and political structures in the USSR and Eastern Europe to be sustained indefinitely. The majority of the RCP leadership had already anticipated the direction eventually taken by the FI. Jock Haston unsuccessfully argued on their behalf at the Congress that 'the economies of these countries are being brought into line with that of the Soviet Union' (quoted in Bornstein and Richardson 1986b: 217). In the event, the IS began to slide in the same direction within a few months of the Congress. The precipitant proved to be Yugoslavia's break with the Soviet bloc in June 1948. The IS reacted on 1 July with an 'Open Letter to the Communist Party of Yugoslavia' which declared: 'You hold in your hands a mighty power if only you persevere on the road of socialist revolution', and noted in conclusion 'the promise of victorious resistance by a revolutionary workers' party against the Kremlin machine . . . Long live the Yugoslav Socialist Revolution' (quoted in Hallas 1969: 29).

The camel had got its nose under the tent. If it was conceded in one case that a Stalinist party – whose general secretary, Tito, boasted of his firm way of dealing with 'Trotsky-fascists' as he was breaking with Moscow (Cliff 1982: 67–8) – could carry out a 'socialist revolution', why should this not also have occurred in the rest of Eastern Europe? It took another three years for Pablo, Mandel and Cannon to accept this conclusion and the FI officially to register it. The Third World Congress declared of Eastern Europe in August 1951: '*the structural assimilation of these countries to the USSR must be considered as essentially accomplished and these countries as having ceased to be basically capitalist countries*'. The nationalization of the means of production, as in the case of the USSR, was a necessary and sufficient condition of the existence of workers' states:

> it is above all by virtue of their economic base, . . . characterized by new *production and property relations proper to a statified economy, essentially those of the USSR*, that we have to consider these states as now being *deformed workers' states*.'

Unlike the Soviet Union, the product of an authentic socialist revolution that went wrong, and therefore a *degenerated* workers' state, the Stalinist regimes in Eastern Europe had been born deformed. Thus:

> It has turned out that the revolutionary action of the masses is not an *indispensable condition* needed by the bureaucracy to be able to destroy capitalism under exceptional and analogous conditions and in an international atmosphere like that of the 'cold war'.
>
> (Fourth International 1969a: 54–5)

Since one main consideration involved in drawing this conclusion was the desire to preserve the integrity of Trotsky's analysis of the USSR, proponents of the move were quick to point out that he had envisaged the possibility that the Stalinist bureaucracy might itself do away with capitalism (see, for example, Hansen 1969: 30–2). After the Soviet-German partition of Poland in September 1939 Trotsky (1973c: 18) predicted that

> in the territories scheduled to become a part of the USSR, the Moscow government will carry out through the expropriation of the large landowners and statification of the means of production. This variant is most probable not because the bureaucracy remains true to the socialist programme but because it is neither desirous nor capable of sharing the power, and the privileges the latter entails, with the old ruling classes in the occupied territories.

Trotsky (1973c: 18) compared '[t]his measure, revolutionary in character – "the expropriation of the expropriators" ', but 'achieved in a military-bureaucratic fashion', to the abolition of serfdom in Poland by Napoleon's occupying forces. Socialist revolution apparently could, like bourgeois revolution, be imposed from above. Trotsky (1973c: 19) nevertheless went on to qualify this judgement:

> The primary political criterion for us is not the transformation of property relations in this or another area, however important these may be in themselves, but rather the change in the consciousness and organization of the world proletariat, the raising of their capacity for defending former conquests and accomplishing new ones. From this one, and the only decisive standpoint, the politics of Moscow, taken as a whole, completely retains its reactionary character and remains the chief obstacle on the road to world revolution.

This passage highlights the difficulty in which Trotsky's identification of a workers' state with a statized economy left his 'orthodox' heirs. His objective was the kind of revolution envisaged by Marx and Lenin, and which had occurred, at least briefly, in 1917, in which the working class broke up the old state apparatus and replaced it with one under workers' direct and democratic control. It was from this perspective that 'the consciousness and organization of the world proletariat' was 'the only decisive standpoint', one from which Stalinism was condemned as 'reactionary'. But if the Russian bureaucracy could 'expropriate the expropriators', not just in parts of Poland, but throughout Eastern Europe, surely this was of more weight practically to those wishing to get rid of capitalism than the aspiration, perhaps Utopian, towards socialism from below? Trotsky himself tended, in response to criticisms of his analysis of the USSR, to describe the classical Marxist conception of a workers' state, based on soviet democracy and open competition among parties, as a 'norm', from which the Stalin regime was a deviation produced by particular historical circumstances (see, for example, Trotsky 1976b: 60–71). But Trotsky, a good pupil of Hegel and Marx, also followed them in rejecting the distinction between values and facts (Trotsky *et al.* 1973). The self-emancipation of the working class might prove to be little more than a norm incapable of realization and therefore politically irrelevant.

It was Pablo who drew the FI in this direction in the early 1950s. The intensification of conflict between the Eastern and Western blocs which reached its climax in the outbreak in 1950 of a limited 'hot' war in Korea placed a Third World War firmly on the agenda.

Pablo (1974a: 7) argued that this would be 'an *international civil war*', between world capital and labour, represented respectively by the Western powers and the Stalinist states, '*Revolution-War*', '*War-Revolution*'. This prospect should be welcomed by Trotskyists, since world war would accelerate '*the process already initiated of the convulsive transformation of our society which would be abated only with the triumph of socialism*' (Pablo 1974a: 9). The fact that the 'War-Revolution' could occur under Stalinist leadership should not give the FI pause since

> the transformation of capitalist society into socialism . . . will probably take an entire historical period of several centuries and will in the meantime be filled with forms and regimes transitional between capitalism and socialism and necessarily deviating from 'pure' forms and norms.
>
>   (Pablo 1974a: 10)

The FI's sections would be best placed to influence events if they entered the social-democratic and even Communist parties since they could not 'be smashed and replaced by others in the relatively short time between now and the decisive conflict' and, moreover, would '*develop centrist tendencies which will lead for a whole stage of the radicalization of the masses and of the objective revolutionary processes in their respective countries*' (Pablo 1974b: 35). Entrism now meant, not the kind of raiding party for members involved in the 'French turn' of the mid-1930s (see Section 1.3 above), but what Pablo called 'entry *sui generis*', a long-term involvement in the mass working-class parties in order to encourage and influence the development of centrist tendencies vacillating between reform and revolution.

At least in its practical conclusions this policy corresponded quite closely to what the British supporters of the IS had been doing for some years. As part of a process which led effectively to the destruction of the RCP and the abandonment of revolutionary politics by some of its ablest leaders, notably Haston, a minority led by Gerry Healy was permitted in 1947, at the insistence of the IS, to organize separately from the RCP majority and to enter the Labour Party. The demoralization and disorientation of the majority as a result of both internal disagreements and the difficulty of sustaining an independent organization in conditions of economic boom and a reforming Labour government, led them to decide two years later to disband the RCP and enter the Labour Party, where they were compelled by the IS to submit to Healy's authority. Healy, in what proved to be the beginning of a long career as the Witchfinder-General of British Trotskyism, proceeded to purge 'the Club' (as the British section was now known), of those of an independent mind, particularly the supporters of such RCP leaders as Cliff and Grant. Meanwhile, Healy and his chief ally, John Lawrence, produced an entrist paper, *Socialist Outlook*, in collaboration with left-wing Labour Members of Parliament, who could agree that the Cold War was a straightforward conflict between the 'progressive bloc' and Western imperialism. (See, on the decline and fall of the RCP, Bornstein and Richardson 1986b: chs 6 and 7.)

Although the SWP leadership had been heavily implicated in the dismemberment of the RCP, and in a similar IS intervention in France which reduced the PCI to a rump led by the loyal Pierre Frank, Pablo's apparent demotion of the Trotskyist movement to an adjunct of Stalinism was too much for them to swallow. Cannon (1973a: 80) quoted a member of the Chicago branch who asked: 'If there are going to be centuries of Stalinism, what's the sense of my going out and selling ten papers on the street corner?' Like her, Cannon baulked at a logic which seemed to deprive the existence of independent Trotskyist organizations of any point. The American, French, and British sections became bitterly divided by disputes central to which was the issue of 'Pabloism'. Finally, in 1953 the IS and the SWP parted company. Cannon, and his British and French allies, led respectively by Healy and by Pierre Lambert, formed the separate International Committee of the Fourth International (IC) in opposition to the IS led by Pablo, Mandel, and Frank. The disintegration of orthodox Trotskyism into rival would-be 'Internationals' proved permanent. The SWP and the IS did in fact succeed in organizing a 'Reunification Congress' in June 1963, which established the United Secretariat of the Fourth International (USFI), but the titles proved hollow. The reconciliation involved the SWP shedding Healy and Lambert. Healy's Socialist Labour League (SLL) – later renamed the Workers' Revolutionary Party (WRP) – objected strongly to the claim, made by both the SWP and the IS, that the Cuban Revolution of 1959 had established a new deformed workers' state. The SLL and Lambert's Organisation Communiste Internationaliste (OCI, later PCI) kept the IC going till 1971, when they too quarrelled and formed their own

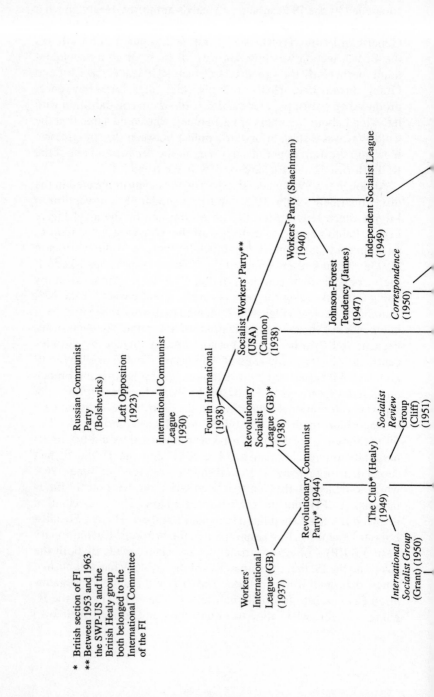

Russian Communist
Party
(Bolsheviks)

Left Opposition
(1923)

International Communist
League
(1930)

Fourth International
(1938)

Socialist Workers' Party**
(USA)
(Cannon)
(1938)

Revolutionary
Socialist
League (GB)*
(1938)

Workers' Party (Shachtman)
(1940)

Johnson-Forest
Tendency (James)
(1947)

Independent Socialist League
(1949)

Correspondence
(1950)

Revolutionary Communist
Party* (1944)

Workers'
International
League (GB)
(1937)

The Club* (Healy)
(1949)

*Socialist
Review
Group
(Cliff)
(1951)*

*International
Socialist Group
(Grant) (1950)*

* British section of FI
** Between 1953 and 1963
the SWP-US and the
British Healy group
both belonged to the
International Committee
of the FI

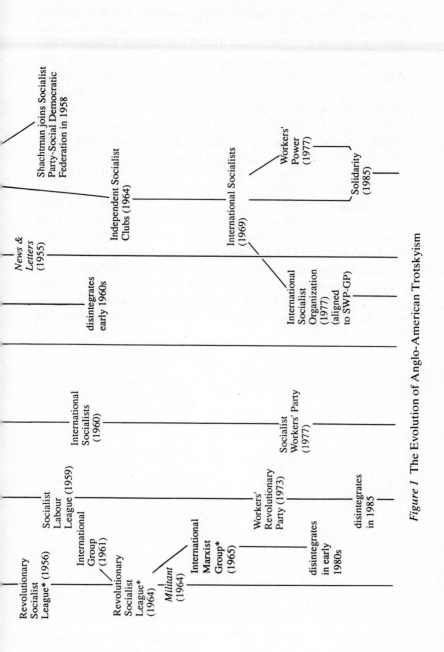

Figure 1 The Evolution of Anglo-American Trotskyism

separate groupings. Meanwhile, Pablo had fallen out with Mandel and Frank, who did not see quite as much socialist potential in the Algerian Revolution as he did. The 'Reunification Congress' was thus preceded by the departure of Pablo's sometime ally, the Argentinian Juan Posadas, and followed by his own expulsion. Even the international regroupment achieved by the disposal of Pablo proved to be something of a pyrrhic victory. From the late 1960s the USFI suffered from chronic divisions, above all between a majority based particularly in the European sections and led by Mandel and the American SWP and its supporters.

This process of fragmentation – of which the previous paragraph is an incomplete and greatly simplified summary, as is the accompanying diagram (see Fig. 1) which traces its course in the USA and Britain – should not conceal the fact that the parties to the various disputes shared certain crucial assumptions, in particular the belief that the USSR, China and Eastern Europe had broken with capitalism and begun, albeit in a bureaucratically deformed manner, the transition to socialism. These assumptions give orthodox Trotskyism certain essential features which underlie, and help explain, its infinite sectarian differences. These form the subject of the next chapter.

Orthodoxies

3.1 Uncritical positivism and uncritical idealism

Marx writes in the *Economic and Philosophic Manuscripts of 1844* that even Hegel's *Phenomenology of Spirit* contains implicit within in it 'the uncritical positivism and the equally uncritical idealism of Hegel's later works – that philosophic dissolution and restoration of the existing empirical world' (Marx and Engels 1975: 332). The thought is that by making Absolute Spirit, a hypostatization of human mental life, the subject of history Hegel prevents the categories of his dialectic from obtaining any critical purchase on the world. Thought and reality, so abruptly fused in the Absolute, the identical subject-object of both nature and history, fall asunder, so that thought, supposedly omnipotent over reality, in fact (as Wittgenstein put it) leaves everything as it is. An analogous oscillation between 'uncritical positivism' and 'uncritical idealism' can be seen at work in orthodox Trotskyism.

Orthodox Trotskyism was constituted, as we saw in the previous chapter, by the decision to preserve Trotsky's analysis of the USSR as a degenerated workers' state by extending it to China and Eastern Europe. This move was in fact merely the most important instance of a powerful drive to defend his thought from refutation. Cannon's denial in November 1945 that the Second World War was over in order to avoid admitting that Trotsky's prediction that the Stalin regime would not survive the war was an extreme case of the same drive, but there are many other examples of a similar tendency. Thus Mandel in 1951 seized on Pablo's prediction of a 'War-Revolution' that would settle the hash of both Stalinism and capitalism to argue that '[t]he period elapsing between the Second and Third World Wars will appear in history as a temporary interlude, and the prediction of Trotsky that the bureaucracy would not survive a war would find itself historically confirmed' (Germain 1974: 23).

Thus seeking to immunize Trotsky's theories from refutation carried with it the danger of transforming them into a set of dogmas. All too frequently this danger was realized. The Transitional Programme drafted by Trotsky and adopted at the First Congress of the FI in 1938 became an especial object of veneration. This document was thus named because it contained a set of 'transitional demands' – for example, the indexation of wages to prices ('the sliding scale of wages'). These were intended to bridge the old division in the Second International before 1914 between the minimum programme of limited reforms attainable within a capitalist context and the maximum programme whose implementation would require the establishment of worker's power. Trotsky argued that the economic crisis was so acute that the struggle for even the most modest improvement in working-class conditions would come into conflict with the capitalist system itself. By agitating for transitional demands the FI would draw around it workers who would discover in the course of their efforts to realize these demands the limitations of reformism. Thus Trotsky described the transitional demands as 'stemming from today's conditions and today's consciousness of wide layers of the working class and unalterably leading to one final conclusion: the conquest of power by the proletariat' (Reisner 1973: 183). The idea was not a new one – Lenin's slogan 'Bread, Land, and Peace' is probably the best example of a transitional demand – and the early Comintern sought to make it the basis of the Communist parties' daily agitation. Trotsky does not seem to have been especially strongly committed to the particular demands contained in the Transitional Programme, and stressed the importance of being able 'to put forward at the right moment sharp, specific, fighting slogans that by themselves don't derive from the "programme" but are dictated by the circumstances of the day and lead the masses forward' (Trotsky 1973e: 143). This warning was generally ignored by orthodox Trotskyists, who tended rather to treat the detailed demands outlined in the Transitional Programme as unalterable. This went along with a propensity to make a fetish of the idea of 'The Programme' itself: its presence or absence was treated as the decisive factor determining whether or not a particular movement would realize the revolutionary potential attributed to it. Typically involved in these attitudes was a refusal to contemplate the possibility that Trotsky was mistaken in assuming that future capitalist economic expansion was ruled out. This bred an economic catastrophism of which Healy and his followers provide the classic case. Throughout the 1950s and 1960s they ignored the abundant evidence of a world-wide boom to announce an imminent, and drastic slump. For the Healyite WRP the actual onset of global recession in the early 1970s was greeted with a fervour almost comparable to that of a Christian fundamentalist in the face of the Second Coming.

It is perhaps appropriate here to consider why it was that the Trotskyist movement should so often have displayed the characteristics of religious sectaries. One could plausibly argue that it is generally true of radical movements in adverse circumstances that they dissolve into disputatious fragments. Christopher Hill has, for example, traced the complex process through which English revolutionaries sought to cope with the rule of Cromwell's major-generals and the Restoration – internal disintegration (the Fifth Monarchists), accommodation (the Harringtonians), retreat into political quietism (the Quakers) or into art (Milton) (Hill 1984). Certainly we can see many analogies with what happened to the Trotskyist movement from the 1940s onwards. Furthermore, the inability to influence events is itself likely to encourage splits: since there is no way of settling differences in analysis or policy by practical tests, why not break away? By transforming the theoretical basis of the movement into a set of irrefutable dogmas orthodox Trotskyism strengthened this temptation. Each distinct current sought to establish itself as the sole authentic interpreter of the tradition's founding texts. Orthodox Trotskyism was further disabled by the idea of the Fourth International itself. Its predecessor and model, the Comintern, had been based on the Bolsheviks' ability, as the leaders of a successful revolution, to rally a substantial portion of the Western labour movement to the new International. The Comintern was thus a mass organization, at whose first three congresses (1919–21) at least the views of its predominantly Russian leadership were challenged and criticized in the light of the experience of the Communist parties' attempts, sometimes successful, to influence the huge social conflicts of the time (Hallas 1985).

The pretensions of a political current numbering a few thousands to be such an International had a crippling effect on the Trotskyist movement, in particular encouraging delusions of grandeur in the 'unknown men' who took charge of the IS in the mid-1940s as the leaders of the 'World Party of the Socialist Revolution'. The attempt to follow events in many countries, integrating them into a global perspective and offering detailed tactical advice to local groups, was something which Trotsky could more or less pull off, though at a price, but, continued by his epigoni, it invited the disasters which actually occurred in the late 1940s and early 1950s. The result was the absurdity of a plethora of groupings, usually with a few hundred members apiece, each claiming either to be, or to be engaged in the 'reconstruction' of, the Fourth International. Hardly more inviting was the alternative pursued by the USFI after 1963 of seeking to prevent further splits while hanging on to the fiction of the Fourth International by endless compromises which sought to hold together political tendencies (respectively the supporters of Mandel and of the American SWP) which often seemed to have little left in common.

One consequence of making a theory immune to refutation is that, as Popper (1969: ch. 1) pointed out, it is then consistent with any set of observations. The obverse of a dogmatism so rigid as to ignore any contradictory evidence is a flexibility so supple that it can incorporate everything into its framework, at the price of explaining nothing. Ernest Mandel is probably the best example of this tendency within orthodox Trotskyism. A brilliant and prolific writer and orator, especially skilled in debate, Mandel has, by the scope and erudition of his major economic treatises – *Marxist Economic Theory, Late Capitalism, The Second Slump* – lent a much needed prestige to the USFI, whose main leader he has been for the past quarter-century. There is in fact an organic connection between Mandel's conception of scientific method, as elaborated and applied in his economic writings, and his defence of Trotskyist orthodoxy. In *Late Capitalism*, his main attempt to account for the long post-war boom and its subsequent collapse into crisis at the end of the 1960s, Mandel rejects a 'monocausal' theory of the evolution of capitalism. On the contrary,

> up to a certain point *all* the basic variables of this mode of production
> can partially and periodically perform the role of autonomous

variables – naturally not to the point of complete independence but in
an interplay constantly articulated through the laws of development
of the whole capitalist mode of production.

(Mandel 1975: 39)

He lists six such variables – the organic composition of capital; the
distribution of constant capital between fixed and circulating
capital; the rate of surplus-value; the rate of accumulation; the
turnover time of capital; and the relationship between Departments
I and II, the sectors producing capital and wage goods, respectively
– and much of the book is devoted to exploring the way in which
these variables shaped the post-war world economy.

The difficulty, particularly from the point of view of Marxism's
aspiration to be a theory of the social totality, is that Mandel
provides no general account of the relative importance of the
variables. This does not seem consistent with Marx's (1973: 101)
own 'method of rising from the abstract to the concrete', which
treats certain features of the economy as more fundamental than
others, and it is indeed remarkably close to the 'theory of
self-contained factors' vigorously denounced by Trotsky (for example, 1981: 389ff.). Substantively, Mandel's stress on multiple
causality leads at times to a syncretism perhaps most evident in his
unsuccessful attempt to integrate the idea of long waves of
economic development (most fully formulated by Kondratiev) with
Marx's theory of the tendency of the rate of profit to fall (see
Harman 1978). One advantage, however, of this preference for
pluricausal explanation is that apparent refutations can be dealt
with through the discovery of some additional, hitherto ignored,
factor. Mandel applies all the subtle skills of a medieval schoolman
to distinguishing relevant factors – for example, identifying no less
than five distinct wars within the Second World War (Mandel 1986:
45). The effect is to deprive social theory of the interaction with
potentially disconfirming observations. Thus, Mandel (1979b: 171)
argues that Trotsky was mistaken in his 'short-term predictions'
rather than in 'his understanding of the grand lines of development
of our century'. Stalinism and capitalism did go into crisis, albeit in
the 1960s and 1970s rather than at the end of the Second World
War. It is as if Trotsky's theory were a film which, when first shown,
was run too fast. Slowed down to the proper speed, the film is fine.
This hardly accords with the urgency of Trotsky's predictions, his

insistence on the temporary and parasitic character of the Stalin regime, his claim that if the war did not issue in revolution Marxism itself would stand refuted. A theory thus denied any friction with experience is likely, not to anticipate events, but always to lag behind them, preserving its integrity at the price of the loss of any explanatory power.

3.2 The big battalions

The paradox of orthodox Trotskyism is that, by seeking to preserve the letter of Trotsky's theory, it deprived the latter of much of its substance. This is clearest politically with respect to the agency of socialist revolution. Trotsky, in line with his general commitment to classical Marxism, conceived socialism as the self-emancipation of the working class. But if the Eastern European countries were deformed workers' states, then forces other than the proletariat could carry through socialist revolution. Trotsky (n.d.: 56) had, in his polemic against Lenin's conception of the party after the 1903 Congress, identified the danger of 'substitutionism': 'The group of "professional revolutionaries" was not marching at the head of the conscious proletariat, it was acting in . . . in place of the pro-letariat.' Trotsky later accepted Leninism as consistent with pro-letarian self-emancipation, but, in their disarray after 1945, many of his followers were drawn towards substitutionism – not that they were in any position to supplant the working class, but they attached their hopes to forces acting in its name.

Pablo's policy of long-term 'entry *sui generis*' into the Communist parties (see Section 2.2 above) was one example of this tendency. But the greatest temptation came in the case of those revolutions, in what we now call the 'Third World', where Stalinist movements led peasant armies to victory around a programme of national rather than social liberation – Yugoslavia, China, Cuba and Vietnam. On the face of it, these upheavals might be thought to count as a refutation of the theory of permanent revolution, according to which backward countries can only defeat imperialism where the working class assumes leadership of the national struggle and breaks with capitalism (see Section 1.1 above). The response of the FI leadership was rather to assert the contrary. Thus the Third World Congress declared in 1951: 'The dynamics of the Yugoslav revolution confirms the theory of the permanent revolution on all points' (Fourth International 1969b: 57). Just because this and later such revolutions had secured national independence and carried extensive land reforms or nationalizations, they must have been carried out under the leadership of the working class. The alternative – that the theory of permanent revolution was false or at least required modification – was simply too much even to consider. Other inconvenient developments – the relatively peaceful disintegration of the European colonial empires and the transformation of some Third World states into newly industrializing countries – were disposed of by asserting that these changes failed to meet Trotsky's insistence that 'the *complete and genuine solution* (not the *beginning* of a solution) of the tasks of the bourgeois-democratic revolution' could be achieved only by the proletarian overthrow of capitalism (Mandel 1979b: 73; see also Löwy 1981; Callinicos 1982b).

Characterizing the great post-war Third World revolutions as socialist might preserve Trotskyist orthodoxy, but at the price of introducing new difficulties. For one thing, as Michael Löwy (1981: 214) acknowledges, in all these cases 'not only was the proletariat not directly the social agent of revolution, but *the revolutionary party was not the direct, organic expression of the proletariat*'. Nevertheless, the Vietnamese, Chinese and Cuban Communist parties 'were the *political and programmatic* expression of the proletariat by virtue of their adherence to the historic interests of the working class' and the fact that their '*ideologies* were proletarian' (Löwy 1981: 214–15). So a movement can be proletarian even if it contains very few workers among its members and has no involvement in the everyday life and struggles of the proletariat. The scope thus offered for substitutionism is clear enough, particularly when we recall that the 'proletarian ideologies' of these movements were variants of the Stalinist 'Marxism-Leninism' which Trotsky so unremittingly attacked as vulgarized and debased distortions of the revolutionary socialist tradition. This entire line of reasoning irresistibly calls to mind Brecht's famous poem after the 1953 Berlin rising, in which he suggests that the East German government should dissolve the people and elect another one in its place.

But even granted the proletarian character of the Yugoslav, Chinese and Vietnamese Communist parties, and (even more dubiously) of the 26 July Movement in Cuba, which only espoused Marxism-Leninism after the 1959 Revolution, there remained another more fundamental problem: how could Stalinism, dubbed by Trotsky counter-revolutionary on a world scale, overthrow capitalism in these instances? The answer was simplicity itself: these movements were not Stalinist after all. As Mandel (1983: 54) put it:

> The dictatorship of the proletariat was established in Yugoslavia, China, Vietnam, and Cuba by *pragmatic revolutionary leaderships* that had a revolutionary practice but a theory and programme that was adequate neither to their own revolution, nor especially to the world revolution.

Neither Stalinists nor 'revolutionary Marxists', Tito, Mao, Ho and Castro – were 'left centrists', whose 'lack of a correct programme' had 'negative practical consequences'; nevertheless, '[t]he fact that they carried out a socialist revolution . . . is infinitely more important than their lack of an adequate theory' (Mandel 1983: 54).

'Centrism' is the name given by Lenin and Trotsky to those socialist currents characterized by their vacillation between reform and revolution, the classic instances being Karl Kautsky and the Austro-Marxists. How then could 'left centrists' carry through socialist revolutions in parts of the Third World? Answers to this question tend to lay great stress on objective circumstances, what Löwy (1981: 158) calls 'the logic of the revolutionary process itself'. Thus Pierre Rousset (1975) argues that a combination of socio-economic pressures and national tradition (notably Confucianism) allowed the Vietnamese Communists to break 'empirically' with Stalinism and carry through the anti-colonial revolution to its finish. No doubt such factors must be taken into account in any explanation of the Vietnamese Revolution, but these hardly encourage one to describe it as a socialist revolution, at least from the standpoint of classical Marxism, which places such a strong stress on the self-conscious character of such transformations. History instead operates according to Hegel's ruse of reason, bringing about socialist revolutions whose agents are largely unaware of what they are doing. In Trotsky's (1976a: 349) own words, 'the permanent character of the revolution thus becomes a law placing itself above history, independent of the policy of the leadership and of the material development of revolutionary events'.

In any case, if 'pragmatic revolutionary leaderships' can get rid of capitalism in large parts of the Third World, what is the point of the Fourth International? In some variant or another, this difficulty had been around since the late 1940s but was rendered more acute by the Nicaraguan Revolution of 1979. The American SWP greeted this event, along with the Cuban Revolution and the coup which, also in 1979, placed the ill-fated regime of Maurice Bishop in power in Grenada, as 'the re-emergence of proletarian revolutionists in power – for the first time since the Stalinist-led bureaucracy put an end to such leadership in the Soviet Union and expunged proletarian internationalism from the Communist International more than half a century ago' (Barnes 1983: 10). The appearance of this 'revolutionary Marxist current, . . . living and struggling to extend the socialist revolution today' (Barnes 1980: 30) conjures up the prospect of 'a worldwide political convergence of forces' which might unite the Cuban Communist Party, the Sandinistas *and* the USFI in 'a mass, communist International' (Barnes 1983: 77). Moreover, American SWP leader Jack Barnes (1983: 69) argues, Trotskyism is itself an obstacle to this 'convergence', since 'probably 80 per cent of those on a world scale who present themselves as Trotskyists . . . are irreformable sectarians'. The roots of this sectarianism are to be found in Trotsky himself, since the theory of permanent revolution rules out the possibility of the establishment of 'workers' and farmers' governments', representing 'a stage in the class struggle where capitalist property relations have not yet been abolished, but workers and farmers have conquered political power through a genuine revolution' (Barnes 1983: 35). The Cuban, Nicaraguan and Grenadan Revolutions all passed through such a stage preliminary to the establishment of the dictatorship of the proletariat, a change involving primarily the nationalization of the means of production, which occurred only in Cuba.

These arguments represented the most dramatic example of the drift to Stalinism which had been a constant temptation for orthodox Trotskyists since the late 1940s. The idea of 'workers' and farmers' governments' in particular was strikingly reminiscent of Lenin's old formula of the 'revolutionary-democratic dictatorship of the proletariat and peasantry' which Trotsky had so forcefully criticized after the 1905 Revolution and then again in the debates of the 1920s (see Section 1.1 above). The American SWP, indeed, swiftly developed a style of political analysis strongly reminiscent of Pablo's division of the world into 'progressive' Eastern and reactionary Western blocs in the early 1950s (see Section 2.3

above). This whole change of direction was strongly resisted by
Mandel and his supporters within the USFI (see, for example,
Mandel 1983). But these efforts could not conceal the fact that the
American SWP under Barnes had simply drawn the consequences
of orthodox Trotskyism. Both sides were agreed that proletarian
revolutions had occurred without the proletariat taking any active
part. It mattered little whether the makers of these revolutions were
called 'revolutionary Marxists' or 'pragmatic revolutionaries' or
even 'Stalinists'. If they could achieve socialism from above,
without workers' councils taking power, then Trotskyism had lost
its *raison d' être*. Not even all Mandel's formidable forensic skills
could conceal this simple fact (Callinicos 1984).

Orthodox Trotskyists outside the USFI have attempted similar
balancing acts to Mandel's, with equal lack of success. When the
British RCP anticipated the FI's development by declaring the
Eastern European 'buffer zone' workers' states in 1947–8 (see
Section 2.2 above), Ted Grant had formulated the concept of
'proletarian Bonapartism'. This was an interesting example of what
Lakatos (1976: 20ff., 83ff., 93ff.) called 'concept-stretching', where
a theory is defended from refutation by the extension of its concepts
to cover apparently aberrant cases. Marx had coined the term
'Bonapartism' to describe regimes where the state, while not
controlled by the bourgeoisie, acted in the latter's class interests
(Draper 1977: Bk II). Grant (1989: 231), following but developing
formulations of Trotsky's, extended the concept from capitalist to
workers' states, and advanced the general proposition that '[f]or
quite a lengthy period, *there can be a conflict between the state and
the class which that state represents*'. 'Stalinism', Grant (1989: 302)
argued, 'is a form of Bonapartism that bases itself in the institution
of state ownership, but it is different from the norm of a workers'
state as fascism or bourgeois Bonapartism differs from the norm of
bourgeois democracy'. On this basis, Grant (1989: 350) was more
generous than the USFI about the successes of 'proletarian
Bonapartism' in the Third World, in 1978 describing China, Cuba,
Vietnam, Laos, Cambodia, Syria, Angola, Mozambique, Aden,
Benin, and Ethiopia as deformed workers' states. Although
criticized by other orthodox Trotskyists, the list reflected Grant's
relatively consistent use of statization of the economy as the
criterion of the existence of a workers' state. He resisted, however,
the temptation to welcome the makers of these revolutions into the

Trotskyist camp – for example, in 1949 attacking the IS's treatment of Tito as 'an unconscious Trotskyist' (Grant 1989: 298). The pressure towards substitutionism nevertheless found political expression. Having joined the Labour Party with the rest of the RCP majority in 1949, Grant became the principal figure of the Militant Tendency, which emerged as the strongest organized left grouping inside the Labour Party at the end of the 1970s. Practising a far more long-term version of entrism than anything envisaged by Trotsky, Militant supporters expected catastrophic economic crisis to radicalize the Labour Party and provide mass support for a left government which would effect '[a]n entirely peaceful transformation of society' by means of large-scale nationalization authorized by Parliament through an Enabling Act (Taaffe 1986: 25 and *passim*). On this scenario, a transformed social democracy would play the kind of role which other orthodox Trotskyists thought some versions of Stalinism would perform (McGregor 1986).

3.3 Into the watch-tower: Deutscher and Anderson

The contradictions discussed in the previous section all derive from the effort to uphold Trotsky's analysis of the USSR as a workers' state, at the price of effectively recognizing Stalinism as a revolutionary force, while seeking at the same time to maintain an independent Trotskyist movement. There were two ways out of the dilemma involved – to abandon the theory of degenerated and deformed workers' states, as the tendencies discussed in Chapters 4 and 5 did, or to give up the project, formulated by Trotsky in 1933, of building revolutionary organizations independent of Stalinism and social democracy. The most distinguished representative of the latter alternative is Isaac Deutscher. Deutscher's formidable literary gifts – Perry Anderson (1984b: i) calls him 'one of the greatest socialist writers of this century' – were demonstrated above all in his classic biography of Trotsky, which played a major role in preserving the latter's reputation and introducing the generation radicalized in the 1960s to the classical Marxist tradition. Yet the thrust of Deutscher's writings was fundamentally opposed to the political direction taken by Trotsky after 1933. Active in the Polish Trotskyist group in the 1930s, Deutscher drafted the arguments on which their opposition to the formation of the Fourth International at the 1938 founding conference was based (Reisner 1973: 296–7;

Deutscher 1970c: 421, n. 1). During wartime exile in Britain he drifted out of the Trotskyist movement. Whether cause or consequence of this decision, Deutscher's mature analysis certainly provided it with a rationale.

Shachtman (1962: 270) observed: 'Deutscher is overwhelmingly fascinated – you might also say obsessed – by . . . analogies between the bourgeois revolutions (the French in particular . . .) and the Bolshevik revolution'. These analogies play the function of establishing a broad identity of structure between bourgeois and proletarian revolutions. This identity thus posited is politically important for two reasons. First, Deutscher postulates a general historical law according to which revolutions move from a phase of popular mobilization in which the revolutionaries enjoy mass support to one in which they are compelled by events to establish a minority dictatorship that preserves the conquests of the revolution at the price of repression aimed at, among others, an extreme Left which denounces the betrayal of the original uprising's ideals. The emergence of Stalin, like that of Cromwell and Napoleon before him, was historically inevitable. Moreover, he represented, not the betrayal of the revolution but its continuation. Discussing the methods of compulsion and armed expansion used by the Bolshevik leaders during the Civil War, Deutscher (1970a: 515) traced

> the thread of unconscious historic continuity which led from Lenin's hesitant and shamefaced essays in revolution by conquests to the revolutions contrived by Stalin the conquerer. A similar subtle thread connects Trotsky's domestic policy of these years with the later practices of his antagonist. Both Trotsky and Lenin appear, each in a different field, as Stalin's unwitting inspirers and prompters. Both were driven by circumstances beyond their control and by their own illusions to assume certain attitudes in which circumstances and their own scruples did not allow them to persevere – attitudes which were ahead of their time, out of tune with the current Bolshevik mentality, and discordant with the main themes of their own lives.

Stalin's peculiar virtue lay precisely in his lack of scruple and of sympathy with the classical Marxist tradition, which allowed him to act as 'the guardian and the trustee of the revolution' in its conservative phase, launching at the end of the 1920s the 'second revolution' of collectivization and industrialization (Deutscher 1949: 361, 294) and transforming Eastern Europe after 1945 '"from above and from outside" – by conquest and occupation' (Deutscher 1970c: 257). Here we may note a second aspect of the analogy Deutscher drew between bourgeois and socialist revolutions. The English and French Revolutions were bourgeois, not because capitalists led them – on the contrary, '[t]he leaders were mostly "gentlemen farmers" in England and lawyers, doctors, journalists and other intellectuals in France' – but because of the benefits they brought the bourgeoisie: 'Bourgeois revolution creates the conditions in which bourgeois property can flourish' (Deutscher 1967: 22). Anderson (1966: 232) drew out the implication of extending this feature of bourgeois revolution to its socialist counterpart: 'Capitalism does not automatically or everywhere require a victorious industrial bourgeoisie to launch it – any more than socialism requires a victorious industrial proletariat to impose it.' Much more explicitly than was usual in the orthodox Trotskyist mainstream, Stalinism was thus acknowledged as a revolutionary force and the classical conception of socialism as proletarian self-emancipation abandoned. Deutscher's Trotskyist critics were quick to challenge his identification of bourgeois and socialist revolutions and to argue that the working class, because of its separation from the means of production under capitalism, can only become economically dominant by taking political power (Shachtman 1962: chs 12 and 13; see, more generally, Callinicos 1989).

Stalin becomes, on Deutscher's interpretation of the Russian Revolution, not the aberration which Trotsky regarded him to be, but an instrument of historical necessity. In a revealing passage, Deutscher (1970c: 241–7) invoked Plekhanov, the great theorist of Second International Marxism, to refute Trotsky's 'startling conclusion' that without Lenin the October Revolution would not have occurred. Alasdair MacIntyre (1971: 59) commented: '[W]e can see why this is necessary for [Deutscher's] . . . whole argument. If from time to time history presents us with real alternatives, then I am not just part of an inevitable historical progress' (see also Callinicos 1987a: 79–82). Whereas Trotsky's Marxism, even when he came closest to predicting the inevitable economic breakdown of capitalism in the late 1930s, laid great stress on the 'subjective factor', the role of conscious human agency in transforming society, (see Section 1.3 above), Deutscher preferred to explain events in the light of an unfolding historical necessity. This had direct political consequences. In the post-war world, Deutscher (1970c: 518) argued, 'the class struggle, suppressed at the level on which it had been traditionally waged', was 'fought at a different level and in different forms, as rivalry between power blocs and as cold war'. Though Deutscher's sympathies were with the Soviet bloc in this struggle, he preferred to any form of organized political activity withdrawal to 'a *watch-tower*' from where to 'watch with detachment and alertness this heaving chaos of a world, to be on a sharp lookout for what is going to emerge from it, and to interpret it *sine ira et studio*' (Deutscher 1984: 57–8). The most positive development Deutscher detected from his watch-tower was the emergence in the USSR after Stalin's death of reformers who he expected would carry out from above the political revolution which Trotsky had believed would come from below: Deutscher cast first Beria, then Malenkov, and finally Krushchev in the role of leaders of this revolution (see Cliff 1982: 166–91). Deutscher (1984: 145–6) thus condemned the 1953 Berlin rising – which was concentrated in the working-class areas which had supported the Communists in the Weimar era – as 'objectively counter-revolutionary' because it 'compromised the idea of a gradual relaxation of the Stalinist regime' advocated by such 'reformists' as Beria.

Though Deutscher's adopted role as a critical observer of events ruled out any attempt on his part to build a political organization, his ideas have continued to exert an influence since his death in 1967 as a result of their impact on the gifted group of young British intellectuals who took over the *New Left Review* (*NLR*) in 1962 and transformed it over the following two decades into perhaps the major journal of social theory in English (see, on *NLR's* history, Birchall 1980) Perry Anderson, editor of *NLR* till 1983, is best known for the two volumes of his genealogy of the modern state so far to have appeared (1974a; 1974b). But he is also the main exponent of a Deutscherite version of orthodox Trotskyism. He contrasted Trotskyism to Western Marxism as the continuation of the classical tradition (Anderson 1976: 96–101), and praised it for having 'alone . . . proved capable of an adult view of socialism on a *world* scale' (Anderson 1980: 156). Nevertheless, Anderson maintained a critical distance from the Trotskyist movement – though other *NLR* editors (notably Tariq Ali, Robin Blackburn, and Quintin Hoare) were for much of the 1970s leading members of the USFI's British section, the International Marxist Group. While describing Trotsky's 'fundamental hypotheses' as 'unsurpassed to

this day as a framework for investigation of Soviet society'
(Anderson 1980: 117), Anderson criticized them for depicting
Stalinism as 'merely an "exceptional" or "aberrant" refraction of
the general laws of transition from capitalism to socialism'. On the
contrary, '[t]he structures of bureaucratic power and mobilization
pioneered under Stalin proved both more *dynamic* and more
general a phenomenon on the international plane than Trotsky ever
imagined' (Anderson 1984a: 125–6). Indeed,

> Stalinism . . . proved to be not just an apparatus, but a *movement* –
> one capable not only of keeping power in a backward environment
> dominated by scarcity (USSR), but of actually winning power in
> environments that were yet more backward and destitute (China,
> Vietnam).
>
> (Anderson 1984a: 127)

In line with the contrast between East and West which is one of the
main themes of Anderson's historical writings, it seems that, while a
classical revolutionary strategy remains appropriate in the bourgeois democracies of advanced capitalism (Anderson 1976–7),
Stalinism is the normal form taken by anti-capitalist movements in
the Third World (see, for example, the suspiciously Andersonian
tones of the criticism of the 'sectarian workerism' of the Workers'
Party of Brazil in Sader 1987).

Other *NLR* editors drew eminently Deutscherite conclusions
from this analysis. Thus Fred Halliday (1983) argued that the
Second Cold War that broke out in the late 1970s was a continuation
of Deutscher's 'Great Contest', an 'inter-systemic conflict between
capitalism and communism' in which the sympathies of the Western
Left should be with the Eastern bloc as the embodiment, however
bureaucratically distorted, of the world proletariat in the global
class struggle between capital and labour. And, as tensions between
NATO and the Warsaw Pact were at least temporarily alleviated in
the era of *glasnost* and *perestroika*, Tariq Ali, who acknowledged
the influence of 'Isaac Deutscher, Leon Trotsky and Ernest Mandel
(in that order)', hailed Gorbachev as the agent of 'the political
revolution (which is already under way)' in the USSR, a 'revolution
from above' dictated by the dependence of the Soviet Union's
survival on the 'abolition of the bureaucratic caste' (Ali 1988: ix,
xiii). The connection between these conclusions, which depict the
Stalinist states globally and the reform wing of the Soviet

bureaucracy domestically as progressive forces, and the orthodox Trotskyist theory of bureaucratic workers' states should be clear in the light of the present and preceding chapters. Let us now consider the ideas of those Trotskyists who, in order to avoid such conclusions, rejected the theory.

Heresies

4.1 Max Shachtman and the evil empire

'[W]e are all, on the American Trotskyist left, the children of the 1940 split', the veteran Tim Wolforth (1989: 45) wrote recently. The foundation of the Workers' Party (WP) in April 1940 by Max Shachtman and other dissident leaders of the American SWP (see Section 2.1 above) was indeed to have long-term political consequences (see Fisk 1977 for a history of the Shachtmanite movement). Although the WP formally adhered to the FI till 1948, the idea that the USSR was a new form of class society, bureaucratic collectivism, was to lead Shachtman and most of his followers a long way from Trotskyism, and indeed from the Marxist tradition altogether.

The expression 'bureaucratic collectivism' was in fact coined not by Shachtman, who first adopted it in 1941, but by Bruno Rizzi in 1939. Rizzi (1985: 54) argued that 'the USSR represents a new type of society ruled by a new social class . . . Property, collectivized, effectively belongs to this class which has installed a new and superior system of production.' The relations of production were distinct from those of capitalism and socialism. Indeed, says Rizzi (1985: 80) '[e]xploitation goes on exactly as in a slave society', with '[t]he worker of today's Russia' now displaying 'the characteristics of a slave', reduced to the status of 'livestock which has to be cared for, housed, and whose reproduction is of great concern to the master'. Rizzi (1985: 60) discerned the same pattern emerging in Nazi Germany and Fascist Italy: 'In these regimes a new managerial class, in the process of formation, announces that capital is at the service of the state.' James Burnham, who initially sided with

Shachtman against Trotsky and Cannon in the 1939–40 faction fight but broke with Marxism in the course of the debate (Burnham 1940), developed a very similar analysis to Rizzi's in a celebrated book, *The Managerial Revolution*, first published in 1941. He, too, detected a global tendency, most fully realized in the USSR, to replace capitalism with a new mode of production, 'managerial society', but, more consistent than Rizzi, he drew the conclusion that 'socialism is not possible of achievement or even approximation in the present period' (Burnham 1962: 53). This analysis allowed Burnham to move rapidly to the right and become, by the late 1940s, an advocate of preventive nuclear war against the Soviet Union (Wald 1987: 189–90). Rizzi, a shoe salesman in the late 1930s, seems only to have been on the margins of the Trotskyist movement, and the praise he gave to Hitler and Mussolini for their anti-semitism – 'We must . . . become anti-Jewish because anti-capitalist' – suggests that his true home was on the 'national-revolutionary' left wing of European fascism – though this did not stop him being taken up by Bettino Craxi, leader of the Italian Socialist Party, in the late 1970s (see Westoby 1985).

Shachtman (1962: 291), unlike Burnham and Rizzi, resisted the conclusion that bureaucratic collectivism in Russia represented the wave of the future rather than a 'blind alley'. Indeed, it is striking how much his early writings on the subject simply take over Trotsky's analysis of the Stalin regime, differing chiefly on certain crucial theoretical conclusions. Thus Shachtman agreed with Trotsky that Stalinist Russia was a post-capitalist society rather than a variant of capitalism. State capitalism, in the sense of a society where all the means of production are nationalized but which is still subject to the dynamic of capital accumulation, was an impossibility: 'The norm of capitalism *is* the private ownership of capital' (Shachtman 1962: 279; cf. Trotsky 1970: 245–8). Shachtman, however, disagreed with Trotsky that statization was a sufficient condition of the existence of a workers' state. On the contrary, '[t]he proletariat's relations to property, to the new collectivist property, are indivisibly bound up with its relations to the state, that is, to the political power' (Shachtman 1962: 41). Consequently, '[t]hat political expropriation of the proletariat which is defined in Trotsky's analysis – that is nothing more or less than the destruction of the class rule of the workers, the end of the workers' state' (Shachtman 1962: 46). A workers' state in which, as Trotsky conceded, the working class no longer had political power was a contradiction in terms.

Shachtman was, however, more successful in exposing the inconsistencies in Trotsky's analysis of Stalinism than in replacing it with a better theory. Modes of production are characterized in historical materialism by distinctive forms of surplus-extraction, control over the productive forces, and relations among the exploiters, from which definite tendencies ('laws of motion') may be derived (Callinicos 1987a: ch. 2). Yet no elaborated account of these features of bureaucratic collectivism was forthcoming. Shachtman (1962: 279) followed Rizzi in describing the working class in the USSR as 'the modern slaves, deprived of any political power whatever and therefore of all economic power'. But this claim involved ignoring the very high levels of labour mobility in the USSR, especially during the period of the First Five Year Plan (1928–32), evidence of the existence of a labour market even at the height of the regime's coercion of the mass of population, and exaggerating the importance of the labour camps of the Gulag Archipelago, at their most extensive a secondary feature of the Soviet economy (see, for example, Filtzer 1986). Shachtman's account of the social priorities of production in the USSR was equally unsatisfactory. He wrote: 'In the Stalinist state, production is carried on and extended for the satisfaction of the needs of the bureaucracy' (Shachtman 1962: 58). Trotsky had argued along similar lines, but the implication for Shachtman was that the goal of exploitation under bureaucratic collectivism was, as Marx had argued to be the case under feudalism, ruling-class consumption. The obvious difficulty with such a view was the huge proportion of Soviet national income devoted to the production of capital goods, a reflection of the priority given heavy industry and the military. This pattern in turn indicated the respect in which the rulers of the USSR were themselves subject to pressures deriving from their involvement in the international state system of competing military powers. But such factors played no part in Shachtman's analysis.

These weaknesses of the theory of bureaucratic collectivism – which Tony Cliff (1982: 99) summarized by saying that '[i]t does not define the economic laws of motion of the system, explain its inherent contradictions and the motivation of the class struggle' – gave it an indeterminacy which was to have important political consequences. Shachtman's insistence that the USSR was a new form of class society produced by the contradictions of capitalism, but that socialism nevertheless remained on the agenda as a resolution of these contradictions superior to bureaucratic collectivism, made possible a dramatic political somersault. Initially, the WP remained committed to the conditional defence of the USSR in war, on the grounds that, as its 1941 convention put it, '[f]rom the standpoint of socialism, the bureaucratic collectivist state is a reactionary social order; in relation to the capitalist world, it is on a historically more progressive plane' (quoted in Cliff 1982: 87). After the German invasion of the USSR in June 1941, however, the WP decided to hold a revolutionary defeatist stance, similar to Lenin's during the First World War, on the grounds that Russia had become a 'vassal' of Western imperialism (Cliff 1982: 88–9). Such an argument could not survive what Shachtman (1962: 109ff.) himself described as the Stalinist 'counter-revolutionary revolution' in Eastern Europe. By 1947 Shachtman (1962: 87) was arguing that, far from being more progressive than capitalism, 'Stalinism is precisely one of the forms of barbarism which has manifested itself in the course of the decay of a society which the proletariat has not yet succeeded in lifting onto a rational plane'.

The term 'barbarism' has a very definite sense within the Marxist tradition, being used to refer to forms of social retrogression, declines below the level of productive development hitherto achieved. To call Stalinism the 'new barbarism', as Shachtman (1962: 32) did, therefore implied that socialists should side with capitalism against bureaucratic collectivism, with the higher against the lower form of historical progress. The Shachtmanite group, renamed the Independent Socialist League (ISL) in 1949 in line with lowered post-war expectations, followed this logic in its policies within the American labour movement, where the Communist Party had achieved some influence by the end of the war. Shachtman (1962: 304–6) argued that of the two great enemies of socialism, capitalism and Stalinism, '*inside the working class and its movement, Stalinism is the greater and more dangerous of the two*', '*a reactionary, totalitarian, anti-bourgeois and anti-proletarian* current *in* the labour movement but not *of* the labour *movement*', which could succeed only through 'the crushing of the working class'. Therefore, the ISL should 'prefer the leadership of reformists who aim in their way to maintain a labour movement, to the leadership of Stalinist totalitarians who aim to exterminate it', as part of the process of 'eliminating' the Stalinist 'poison' which 'makes the first claim on the attention of every militant' (Shachtman 1962: 308–9).

This analysis of Stalinism as incipient barbarism very much reflected the mood of part of the Western Left in the 1940s. Already at the end of the 1930s a number of American intellectuals previously sympathetic to Trotskyism, among them Max Eastman, Sydney Hook, and Edmund Wilson, had begun to move in reaction to Stalinism towards social democracy (Burnham and Shachtman 1939). The Nazi victories in the early part of the war encouraged some exiled German Trotskyists to discern the 'development of a modern slave state' as part of a more general process of socio-economic retrogression (IKD Committee Abroad 1943). The triumph of totalitarianism over a decaying civilization is, of course, the central theme of *1984* (Orwell's experiences in the Spanish Civil War had earlier attracted him towards an anti-Stalinist variant of Marxism), but it is also to be found in Norman Mailer's earlier novels – particularly *Barbary Shore*, which reflects his brief flirtation with Trotskyism (see Cannon's (1973b: 212–17) sensible discussion of the novel). Trotsky had detected the political conse-quence of such views – Stalinophobia, leading to support for Western capitalism against the USSR – among his own allies in the faction fight inside the American SWP. At his last meeting with the SWP leadership in June 1940, Trotsky attacked them for a 'passive adaptation' to pro-Roosevelt 'progressives' inside the Teamsters Union and insisted, against Cannon's opposition, that 'the Stalinists are a legitimate part of the workers' movement', 'not at all different from other opposition labour bureaucracies' (Trotsky 1973d: 280, 282). It was, however, Shachtman in the late 1940s who took Stalinophobia to its logical conclusion by arguing that the Western Communist parties were merely the agents of bureaucratic revol-ution. The flaw in this analysis was that it greatly underestimated the tendency, noted by Trotsky (for example, 1974:70–2), for the Communist parties to detach themselves from their subordination to the Russian state, and develop the same kinds of roots, based on control of a trade-union machine, and electoral strategy, as the social-democratic parties – a tendency which became manifest with the emergence of Eurocommunism in the 1970s (for a critique of Shachtman's analysis, see Hallas 1971).

The political import of the argument was much more immediate in the USA of the late 1940s. Shachtman's support for the 'elimination' of Stalinism from the labour movement dovetailed with the drive, central to McCarthyism, to purge the unions of Communist supporters, a necessary condition for the post-war deradicalization of the American working class (see, for example, Davis 1986: ch. 2). So the WP backed Walter Reuther in his struggle to win control of the United Auto Workers from the Communist Party and its allies in 1946–7, an important episode in this process (Fisk 1977: 22–4). This was the beginning of the Shachtmanites' more general identification with the Atlantic alliance against the Eastern bloc. In the late 1940s, disillusionment with the USSR and Cold War hysteria panicked many previously radical metropolitan intellectuals into the arms of the American government. The resulting phenomenon of 'CIA socialism' is summed up by a scene later recalled by Lionel Trilling. At a meeting of the American Committee for Cultural Freedom, Socialist Party leader Norman Thomas rang Allen Dulles, Director of Central Intelligence, successfully to plead for funds to keep the committee going (Bloom 1986: 264). The Shachtmanites were very largely drawn from the milieu of the New York Intellectuals and were therefore heavily influenced by its evolution towards 'liberal anti-communism' (Bloom 1986: chs 10 and 11; Wald 1987: chs 6–9). In 1958 the ISL dissolved itself into the Socialist Party-Social Democratic Federation, which proved to be merely a stage towards entry into the Democratic Party, where Shachtman became a stalwart of the Cold War Right, backing US intervention in Vietnam and even endorsing Richard Nixon in the 1972 presidential election.

A minority led by Hal Draper resisted this evolution, founding in 1964 the Independent Socialist Clubs (ISC), which, swelled by recruits from the student and anti-war movements, became the International Socialists in 1969. But the International Socialists were still bedevilled by the ambiguities of the concept of bureaucratic collectivism which had made Shachtman, in Wolforth's (1988b: 44) words, 'the original theorist of the Evil Empire'. The search for a 'third camp', representing a democratic alternative to both the Viet Cong and the Americans and their allies, prevented the ISC from mounting an effective campaign against the Vietnam war (Fisk 1977: 42–5). From the mid-1970s onwards, however, the International Socialists, along with much of the rest of the American Left, developed a fairly uncritical enthusiasm for Third

World movements such as the Sandinistas, even though these could as plausibly as the Viet Cong be depicted as the agents of bureaucratic collectivist revolution. This made it possible for the International Socialists, along with another grouping of Shachtmanite provenance, Workers' Power, to form, together with dissident members of the American SWP, a new, broader far left organization, Solidarity, in 1985.

The idea that the USSR and its like were post-capitalist class societies has won support outside the Shachtmanite movement, elsewhere on the American Left (for example, Wright 1983) and among dissident Marxists in the Eastern bloc itself (see notably Bahro 1978; Kagarlitsky 1988). But the history of Shachtman and his followers suggests that, in the absence of an articulated theory of the new mode of production, the concept of bureaucratic collectivism has acted primarily as a means whereby its adherents could adapt to the prevailing mood on the local Left.

4.2 C. L. R. James and the virtues of spontaneity

Shachtman shares with orthodox Trotskyism the assumption that, as Ted Grant (1989: 217–18) put it, '*where we have complete statification, quantity changes into quality, capitalism changes into its opposite*'. But there had always been, since the time of the Left Opposition in the 1920s, Trotskyists who challenged this assumption, and argued that the USSR and its replicants represented, not a new mode of production, but a variant of the prevailing one, namely state capitalism. The Johnson–Forest tendency in the United States, so named after the pseudonyms of its two main leaders, C. L. R. James (J. R. Johnson), and Raya Dunayevskaya (Freddie Forest), provided an influential formulation of this idea, arguing in a document submitted to the 1950 convention of the American SWP: 'State-property and total planning are nothing but the complete subordination of the proletariat to capital' (James 1986a: 51). The Johnson–Forest tendency had originally left the SWP with the Shachtmanites in 1940. Reacting however, to the WP's rightward drift, it rejoined the SWP in 1947 but finally broke with the FI in 1950. Thereafter it survived as a small but lively group of workers and students based in Detroit. Originally named *Correspondence*, the group experienced a series of splits, notably in 1955 when Dunayevskaya left to set up her own publication, *News and Letters*,

yet nevertheless exerted a significant if diffuse influence on one of
the most important movements of the 1960s, the League of
Revolutionary Black Workers, which had a major impact on some
of Detroit's auto-plants at the end of the Vietnam war (Georgakas
1986).

C. L. R. James is one of the most important counter-examples to
the charge of Eurocentrism sometimes made against the Trotskyist
movement. In fact, Trotsky's ideas attracted support outside the
advanced capitalist countries from the early years of the Left
Opposition, first of all in China (Wang 1980). The Vietnamese
Trotskyists enjoyed popular support in Saigon until physically
suppressed by the Communist Party in September 1945. Trotskyism
first appeared on the Indian subcontinent during the Second World
War, and was able – though in peculiar conditions and with a tragic
outcome – to become a major force in the politics of Sri Lanka
(Ervin 1988–9). The Trotskyist movement in South Africa provided
the British RCP with some of its main leaders (Ted Grant, Millie
Lee), and has, through the Unity Movement and more recently the
Cape Action League, exerted an enduring influence in the town-
ships of the Western Cape (Callinicos 1988: ch. 4). In the Middle
East Trotskyism attracted such impressive figures as Jabra Nicola, a
leader of the Palestinian Communist Party (see Mandel 1979b: xii;
Cliff 1987:14).

James was, however, in a class all his own. Cricketer, novelist,
historian, theorist, agitator, critic, James, through the diversity of
his talents, the force of his personality, and the power of his oratory,
had a lasting impact on those whose lives he touched (Buhle 1986;
1988). Soon after his arrival in Britain from Trinidad in 1932, he
read Trotsky's *History of the Russian Revolution*, one of the two
books (the other was Spengler's *Decline of the West*) which
converted him to Marxism (James 1983: 270). James joined the
Marxist Group, a Trotskyist group which had entered the Independent Labour Party, in 1934 and rapidly became a leading member,
playing an important role in the campaign against the Italian
invasion of Abyssinia in 1935 (Bornstein and Richardson 1986a: chs
6, 8–10). Trotsky (1971a: 203) had written: 'What characterizes
Bolshevism on the national question is that in its attitude towards
oppressed nations, even the most backward, it considers them not
only the object but also the subject of politics.' This attitude
underlies one main theme of James's work, his concern for the

liberation of colonial peoples, especially in Africa and the African diaspora in the Americas. In the 1930s this was expressed in his work with George Padmore in the International African Service Bureau, a main source of Pan-Africanism (James 1983: 268–70), and in his discussions with Trotsky about how to involve the SWP in the movement for black liberation which both expected to develop in the United States (Trotsky 1972c). But by far James's greatest vindication of black people as agents of their own emancipation rather than as mere victims of oppression was his masterpiece, *The Black Jacobins*, first published in 1938. Here he set the great slave rising of 1791, which transformed Sainte Domingue from a French colony into the Republic of Haiti, in the context of the Atlantic world economy and the French Revolution, demonstrating the interaction between the ebb and flow of popular mobilization in the Caribbean and in Paris, and rescuing from what E. P. Thompson called 'the enormous condescension of posterity' such great black leaders as Toussaint Louverture and Dessalines. A classic of Marxist historiography, *The Black Jacobins* was a major influence on works such as Eric Williams's *Capitalism and Slavery* and an anticipation of the 'history from below' developed by Thompson and other British Marxists after the Second World War. But it was also intended as a political intervention, written amid 'the booming of Franco's heavy artillery, the rattle of Stalin's firing squads and the fierce shrill turmoil of the revolutionary movement striving for clarity and influence' (James 1963: xi), and aimed especially at promoting the struggle for the liberation of Africa from colonial rule (James 1983: 267–8).

James went to the USA in 1938, on a speaking tour for the SWP, and spent the next fifteen years there. It is on this period that his claims to have developed a distinctive version of Marxism must rest. The theory he developed in the Johnson–Forest tendency involved a philosophical method, an analysis of capitalism, and a conception of revolutionary organization. James himself regraded his *Notes on Dialectics*, originally a series of letters on Hegel's *Logic* written to his supporters in 1947, as his most important work (1986b: 165). In fact, the odd brilliant *aperçu* aside, the book is philosophically uninteresting, consisting largely of lengthy extracts from Hegel which James then expounds and seeks to illustrate by applying to debates within the FI. What James chiefly gleaned from Hegel was an aspect of the dialectic frequently criticized by other Marxists, namely the incorporation of all aspects of reality into an integrated whole in such a manner that every event, even the most apparently destructive, could be understood as part of a process striving irresistibly towards its immanent goal (see Callinicos 1983: chs. 1–3). Thus James (1980: 65) told his followers: 'Stalinism is a bitter obstacle. But see it as part of a process.' History at points seemed to James (1980: 97), like Hegel, to be an objective teleology, whose outcome was predetermined, in which 'the inevitability of social-ism' was 'a necessity of logical thinking in dialectical terms'.

Teleological versions of history have often been attractive to revolutionaries in times of defeat such as the late 1940s, since they seem to offer the certainty of eventual victory (Gramsci 1971: 336ff.). But more was involved in James's resort to Hegel. He was concerned to challenge Trotsky's analysis of Stalinism as a tempo-rary aberration whose international influence involved the decep-tion and betrayal of the world working class. Stalinism was rather 'a necessary, an inevitable form of development of the labour movement. The workers are *not* mistaken. They are *not* deceived . . . They are making an experience that is necessary to their own development' (James 1980: 30). The social base of Stalinism was provided by the petty bourgeoisie which, in the era of state capitalism, far from defending private property, sought, with the support of the working class, to abolish it (James 1980: 182ff.). 'As the Social-Democrats were the labour bureaucracy of monopoly capitalism, the Stalinists are the labour bureaucracy of the era of "vast state-capitalist trusts and syndicates"' (James 1986a: 6–7). Far from Stalinist betrayals springing from the pressure of private capital in the West on the Russian bureaucracy, they were a consequence of the establishment of state capitalism in the Soviet Union, itself an extreme case of global tendencies. State capitalism was not a phenomenon exclusive to the USSR and its satellites but a general feature of the world economy West as well as East. Indeed, '[t]he Stalinist bureaucracy is the American [labour] bureaucracy carried through to its ultimate and logical conclusion, both of them products of capitalist production in the epoch of state capitalism' (James 1986a: 43).

Informing this analysis was the belief that 'the new productive system of socialism is primarily distinguished by an entirely new organization of labour *within the process of production itself*, in a reorganization of society beginning in the factory, the centre of production relations' (James 1986a: 31). The failure of Trotsky and his orthodox followers was to rely instead on the abstract criterion of nationalized property, and thus to ignore the basic similarity of the production process in the USSR to that in the West (James 1980: 127ff.). This criticism was part of a more general rejection of Trotsky's thought: 'Trotsky . . . made *no* contribution to the struggle for international socialism. On *every* serious point he was wrong' (James 1980: 137). This disdain for Trotsky seems to date back to James's personal encounters with him. Recalling their meeting in Mexico in April 1939, James (1986b: 166) made the astonishing admission that he 'didn't pay attention' to some of Trotsky's (1974: 249–59) most interesting reflections on the weakness of the FI (see Section 1.1 above). In any case, James (1980: 147) now looked for inspiration to Lenin, whose writings of 1917–23 were 'the greatest possible source of theoretical understanding and insight into the world of today'. James's Lenin was, however, a peculiar one, whose *The State and Revolution* represented the rejection of any vanguard party (James 1980: 140–1). In the epoch of state capitalism, the predominant tendency was for the distinction between the revolutionary party and the working class to break down. James was especially impressed by the Italian Communist Party which, in the late 1940s, had, he claimed, 6–7 million members: 'In Italy already the party is the mass. In this sense the contradiction [between party and class] is on the way to vanishing' (James 1980: 119). Revolutionaries should no longer seek to build vanguard parties on the Bolshevik model. On the contrary, '[t]he task is to abolish organization. The task today is to call for, to teach, to illustrate, to develop *spontaneity* – the free creative activity of the proletariat' (James 1980: 117). James celebrated the Hungarian Revolution of 1956, one of whose 'greatest achievements . . . was to destroy once and for all the legend that the working class cannot act successfully except under leadership of a political party' (James *et al.* 1974: 10). The everyday struggles of workers resisting their exploitation in the factories, manifested for example in the British shop stewards' movement, 'constitute the socialist society and the basic struggle for socialism', which revolutionaries should 'align' themselves with rather than seek to lead (James *et al.* 1974: 113, 125).

This analysis of capitalism, and of 'the emerging socialist society' at work within it in spontaneous shopfloor revolts, reflected James's

Hegelian confidence in a historical process which would inevitably subvert the existing order, using the most unlikely of instruments. This perhaps explains his strange enthusiasm for the Italian Communist Party, whose leaders had systematically suppressed revolutionary impulses among their followers at the end of the Second World War. It may also explain such disastrous misjudgements as his support for Kwame Nkrumah, whom he called 'one of the greatest of living politicians', the 'Lenin' of the African revolution, and his praise of Kenneth Kaunda's 'Humanism' as 'in close harmony with the original conceptions and aims of Marxism' (Buhle 1988: 136–42). James nevertheless remained, till his death, rooted in the Marxist tradition, insisting that '[t]he idea that the emancipation of the workers will be the work of the workers themselves is the literal and total truth' (James *et al.* 1974: 91). He resisted pressures from many of his admirers who, under the influence of black nationalism, argued that black liberation could be achieved only by a movement autonomous of the working class, and argued instead that white workers must be won to the struggle against racism (James and Glaberman 1986). The universality of human emancipation affirmed in *The Black Jacobins* was central to James's thought to the end.

4.3 Cornelius Castoriadis and the triumph of the will

Viewing the USSR as state-capitalist allowed James to re-establish Marx's identification of socialism with the self-emancipation of the working class. He did so, however, in a form which bore a strong resemblance to the 'council communism' of Anton Pannekoek and Hermann Görter, who in the early years of the Comintern challenged the Bolshevik model of socialist revolution, tending instead to attach primacy to the development of workers' councils out of the class struggle at the point of production. The most rigorous version of this response to the crisis of the Trotskyist movement emerged in France from Cornelius Castoriadis and the *Socialisme ou Barbarie* group. Castoriadis – for many years better known under such pseudonyms as Paul Cardan and Pierre Chaulieu – broke with the Greek Communist Party and became a Trotskyist in 1942. After three hazardous years in German- and then British-occupied Athens, he moved at the end of the war to Paris, where he became involved in a faction of the FI French section, the

PCI, which developed parallel to, and in dialogue with, the Johnson–Forest tendency in the US (as late as 1958 Castoriadis contributed to James's key document, *Facing Reality*). In 1949 Castoriadis and Claude Lefort left the FI to found the journal *Socialisme ou Barbarie*. The group around this journal exerted till its dissolution in 1966 an influence quite out of proportion to its size, and counted among its members several figures who were to assume an important role on the Parisian intellectual scene – notably, Castoriadis and Lefort aside, the philosopher Jean-François Lyotard. (See Curtis 1988.)

Like James, Castoriadis argued that Stalinism represented not a historical accident reflecting the pressure of Western capitalism on a backward revolutionary state, but a new phase in capitalist development. Basing themselves on the labour aristocracy and the middle classes, the Communist parties were pursuing 'an equally independent political line and autonomous strategy opposed to that of the bourgeoisie no less than that of the proletariat' (Castoriadis 1988a I, 37). Initially Castoriadis (1988a: I, 50) saw them in terms similar to Shachtman's, as the agents of a 'third historical solution, beyond capitalism and socialism,' 'an unprecedented modern barbarism, entailing an unbridled, rationalized exploitation of the masses, their complete political dispossession, and the collapse of culture'. Subsequently, however, Castoriadis (1988a: I, 67–8) came to the conclusion that the USSR and the other 'socialist countries' represented a form of 'bureaucratic capitalism'. '[T]he continual merger of capital and the state' was a universal tendency, fully operative in the West, but closer to completion in the East, and reflecting 'one identical social and historical need' for

> absolute concentration of the forces of production on the national and international scale, 'planning' of the production that has thus been concentrated, world domination, fusion of the economy with the state, statification of ideology, and the complete reduction of the proletariat to the status of a cog in the productive apparatus.

The culmination of this process of concentration would be the forcible establishment of 'the worldwide domination of a single state' (Castoriadis 1988a: I, 186). In the early 1950s, Castoriadis expected that the Third World War, which he regarded as imminent, would settle the question of which superpower would emerge supreme. He believed that the USSR would enjoy a major advantage in this contest, since its 'relations of production are relations of exploitation expressing the most highly developed form of domination by capital over labour' (Castoriadis 1988a: I, 187), and predicted in 1954 that, given the continuation of present trends, 'Russian production would surpass American production' in a 'relatively short space of time' (Castoriadis 1988a: I, 265).

Castoriadis's use of the expression 'bureaucratic capitalism' to refer to the new socio-economic epoch most clearly represented by Stalinism was in a certain sense misleading. He rejected the concept of state capitalism on the grounds that 'it makes one think that capitalism's economic laws continue to hold after the disappearance of private property, of the market, and of competition, which is absurd' (Castoriadis 1988a: I, 9–10). By contrast, 'bureaucratic capitalism signifies only the extreme development of the most deep-seated laws of capitalism, which leads towards the internal negation of these laws' (Castoriadis 1988a: I, 126). Bureaucratic capitalism was thus capitalism not in the sense of being governed by the laws of motion of the capitalist mode of production formulated by Marx – on the contrary, 'the Russian bureaucratic economy already has freed itself from such laws and now constitutes a new whole that negates capitalism' (Castoriadis 1988a: I, 71) – but in the sense of being the outcome of the operation of these laws, notably the tendency towards the concentration and centralization of capital. Castoriadis increasingly came to see bureaucratic capitalism, in the West as well as the East, as the stage of historical development in which the collective will – primarily of the bureaucracy but also of the working class – supplanted the objective economic processes explored by Marx in *Capital*.

The voluntarist social theory thereby entailed can be seen at three levels of Castoriadis's analysis of bureaucratic capitalism. In the first place, he laid increasing stress on the fact that, in the West, 'the state has a continuous policy of conscious intervention aimed at maintaining economic expansion' (Castoriadis 1988a: II, 234). Keynesian techniques of demand management, made possible by the bureaucratization of 'private' capitalism, had caused the post-war boom. Consequently, rather than being a tendency inherent in the capitalist mode of production, 'economic overproduction crises are a relatively superficial phenomenon belonging merely to one particular phase of capitalism' (Castoriadis 1988a: II, 252). In itself this argument was identical to that of such post-war theoreticians of right-wing social democracy as Anthony Crosland and John Strachey. Castoriadis, however, did not believe that bureaucratic capitalism was less oppressive or irrational than its predecessors. He argued, secondly, that the post-war boom had not overcome 'the fundamental contradiction of capitalism, whether in its private or bureaucratic form, which consists of treating the subject of production as an object' (Castoriadis 1988a: II, 41). The central thrust of capitalist exploitation is strictly to separate the functions of direction and execution, depriving labour of all creativity and concentrating control over the production process exclusively in the hands of management. This project cannot, however, be achieved:

> No modern factory could function for twenty-four hours without this spontaneous organization of work that groups of workers, indepen-dent of the official business management, carry out by filling in the gaps of official production directives, by preparing for the unforeseen and for regular breakdowns of equipment, by compensating for management's mistakes, etc.
>
> (Castoriadis 1988a: II, 68)

The existence of this, the 'true subject of modern production, . . . a *collectivity* of workers' present in the '*elementary groups*' formed spontaneously within the factories 'for the purposes of *production* and . . . for the purposes of *struggle*' (Castoriadis 1988a: II, 166, 167, 169), forms the third theme of Castoriadis's analysis of bureaucratic capitalism. Socialism is merely the self-conscious, organized development of workers' resistance at the point of production, whether this struggle brought them into conflict with the ruling bureaucracy in the East or managers and trade-union officials in the West. Thus, '[t]he *content* of the socialist organiz-ation of society is first of all *workers' management* of production', taking the political form of government by workers' councils, but constituted by 'the *abolition* of *any* separate managerial apparatus and the restitution of such an apparatus to the community of workers' (Castoriadis 1988a: II, 95, 102). Bureaucratic domination was made possible in Russia by the Bolsheviks' failure to maintain the workers'control of production which had developed between the February and October Revolutions (Castoriadis 1988a: I, 97ff.) While 'revolutionary organization' was necessary in the struggle against capital, its form should as far as possible resemble the kind of decentralized democracy that would prevail in the workers' councils (Castoriadis 1988a, II: 213–14). Otherwise it would repeat the pattern whereby the 'organizations created by the working class for its liberation have become cogs in the system of exploitation' (Castoriadis 1988a: II, 193).

Castoriadis' analysis of bureaucratic capitalism enabled *Socialisme ou Barbarie*, like the *Socialist Review* group in Britain (see Chapter 5 below) and the Johnson–Forest tendency in the USA, but unlike the orthodox Trotskyists, to discern one of the most important developments in the West after 1945, the emergence of shopfloor militancy by rank-and-file workers acting independently of their official leaders – a phenomenon at the heart of the social explosions (above all the events of May–June 1968 in France) which announced the end of the post-war boom. By that time, however, Castoriadis had broken with Marxism. This move reflected a contradiction at the heart of his thought. If there was, as he claimed, 'an autonomous movement towards socialism that originates in the workers' struggle against the capitalist organization of production' (Castoriadis 1988a: II, 199), what motivated that struggle in an era when state intervention had rendered economic crisis obsolete? As Castoriadis' (1988a: II, 242–57) criticisms of Marxist economic theory became more radical, he tended to stress capitalism's tendency 'completely [to] bureaucratize society', which, he claimed, 'merely spreads its contradictions everywhere' (Castoriadis 1988a: II, 281, 282). But since, as he noted, the bureaucratization of social life bred apathy and privatization among the Western masses (Castoriadis 1988a: II, 226–7), why not conclude that, as Marcuse was arguing at much the same time, the working class had been integrated into capitalism and therefore lost its revolutionary potential?

Castoriadis resolved this dilemma by radicalizing the voluntarism implicit in his conception of bureaucratic capitalism as the 'internal negation' of capitalism's laws of motion. The class struggle had to be seen as a process in which the actions of labour and capital 'give rise to a historical *creation*, an invention of new forms of organization, of struggle, or of life that in no way were contained in the previous state of affairs' (Castoriadis 1988a: II, 264). In an essay first published in serial form in 1964–5, Castoriadis made this insight the basis of a new philosophy of history. He now explicitly abandoned Marxism, condemning it as an 'objective rationalism' (Castoriadis

1987: 41), whose determinism distorted the real dynamic of social change and whose internal inconsistencies were an increasing embarrassment even to the orthodox. Nevertheless, certain 'intuitions', notably of the young Marx and of Lukács, pointed to a genuinely 'revolutionary element', 'radically opposed' to orthodox Marxism (Castoriadis 1987: 57), which Castoriadis sought to develop. History is not an objective process by the development of the productive forces but the work of the 'the imaginary, which is creation *ex nihilo*', such that change is 'the *positing* of a new type of behavior, . . . the *institution* of a new social rule, . . . the *invention* of a new object or a new form – in short, . . . an emergence or a production which cannot be deduced on the basis of a previous situation' (Castoriadis 1987: 3, 44). The pattern underlying historical processes is not the dialectic of the forces and relations of production, but that arising from the tendency of institutions to become autonomous of society, until broken up by a new creative intervention of the imagination, which itself would inevitably become lost in a fresh process of alienation.

The logic of Castoriadis's (1988a: I, 32ff.) critique of Marxism led him to initiate the dissolution of *Socialisme ou Barbarie* in the winter of 1965–66. His influence as a philosopher and social theorist grew in the 1970s and 1980s. In part this reflected the extent to which his politics now fitted the harsher climate of the Second Cold War, especially in Paris, where the *nouveaux philosophes* led an intellectual reaction against Marxism comparable to that of the New York Intellectuals a generation earlier. Consistent with his earlier view of the USSR as the most advanced form of bureaucratic capitalism, Castoriadis (1988b: 77) depicted the Gorbachev reforms as an 'interlude' in a much longer-term process governed by one overriding goal – 'the accumulation of force in view of external expansion or: Russia as a dominant world power'. But Castoriadis had more to offer than a political analysis highly congenial to Washington neo-conservatives. He developed the philosophy of history first outlined in the mid-1960s, notably in *The Institutional Imagination of Society*, which attracted the praise and criticism of Habermas (1987: 327–35). In fact, this wilfully obscure book is merely one example of a general trend in contemporary social theory, which is to detach Marx's philosophical anthropology from historical materialism and transform it into a general theory of action positing a transhistorical human capacity to overturn social structures.

Anthony Giddens (1981) and Roberto Unger (1987) offer more perspicuous and arguably more interesting versions of this kind of voluntarist social theory. The relevance here of Castoriadis's variant is that his path to it seems to suggest that preserving the commitment to socialism as self-emancipation requires the abandonment of the substance of Marx's theories of history and of capitalism – and perhaps also the acceptance of Western bourgeois democracy. Let us finally consider an attempt to avoid this conclusion.

Reorientations

5.1 Tony Cliff and the theory of state capitalism

Trotsky's political project involved, above all, the attempt to continue the classical Marxist tradition, maintaining its identification of socialism with the self-emancipation of the working class. The last two chapters seem to suggest that this project was, in fact, impossible. Orthodox Trotskyism preserved the letter of Trotsky's writings at the price of depriving them of substance, since forces other than the working class were now regarded as agents of socialist revolution. Those, on the other hand, who challenged Trotskyist orthodoxy – in particular, the idea that the USSR, China, and the Eastern bloc were workers' states – tended subsequently to break with Marxism *tout court*, some, like Shachtman, succumbing to a Stalinophobia so acute as to drive them into the arms of the State Department. The natural conclusion to draw would be that Trotskyism, and with it Marxism itself, was exhausted as an intellectual tradition. At the end of his influential book *After Virtue*, Alasdair MacIntyre (1981: 243–4) recalled Trotsky's claim, in September 1939, that if his predictions of post-war revolution were unfulfilled, Marxism itself would be refuted (see Section 2.2 above): the outcome after 1945 showed that 'Trotsky's own premises entailed that the Soviet Union was not socialist and that the theory which was to have illuminated the path to human liberation had in fact led to darkness'.

This conclusion presumed that Trotsky was correct in presenting the following dilemma: either the Stalinist bureaucracy was an unstable parasitic formation battening off a backward workers' state or it was the ruling class of a new form of society which rendered the class struggle between labour and capital obsolete. But what if this choice did not exhaust the alternatives, if the USSR and its like were a variant of capitalism? The versions of this idea discussed in the last chapter did not develop its possibilities much. James's theory of state capitalism was very little elaborated, while Castoriadis's alternative account of bureaucratic capitalism was in fact much closer to the Burnham–Rizzi–Shachtman concept of bureaucratic collectivism, since it denoted a society no longer governed by the laws of motion of capitalism. It was Tony Cliff who developed a much more articulated theory of state capitalism rooted in *Capital* and the work of later Marxist economists.

Cliff, brought up by Zionist parents in British-ruled Palestine, became a Trotskyist in the mid-1930s. He left Palestine in 1946, and settled in Britain, where he joined the leadership of the RCP. One of his main reasons for coming to Europe was to write a book that would resolve the crisis of post-war Trotskyism by showing that both the Soviet Union and the states of Eastern Europe were degenerated workers' states. After six months' work on the book he came to the conclusion that Trotsky was wrong and that the USSR and the rest of the Eastern bloc were bureaucratic state-capitalist societies. Originally argued in a 1948 RCP internal document that became the basis of Cliff's book, *State Capitalism in Russia*, first published in 1955, this analysis provided the political basis on which the *Socialist Review* group was formed after the expulsion of Cliff's supporters from the FI in 1950 (see Section 2.2 above). The variant of Trotskyism thus founded is generally known as the International Socialist tradition, after the journal *International Socialism*, established in 1960. Most of the groups which identify with this tradition call themselves the International Socialists, although the British group (confusingly enough) has been called the Socialist Workers' Party since 1977. (See Cliff 1987 for an account of his own development and that of the International Socialists/SWP.)

Cliff's theory of state capitalism had two aspects. In the first place, negatively, he sought to establish the falsehood of Trotsky's analysis, focusing on the latter's identification of state ownership with a workers' state:

> From the form of property alone – whether private, institutional or state property – abstracted from the relations of production, it is impossible to define the class character of a social system. For this it is necessary to know the relation between people and the process of

production, the relations between toilers and the means of production . . . 'To try to give a definition of property as of an
independent relation, a category apart – an abstract eternal idea –
can be nothing but an illusion of metaphysics or jurisprudence'
[Marx].

(Cliff 1948: 7)

Cliff provided detailed empirical evidence to show that 'the relation
between people and the control of production' in the USSR was
characterized by the denial to workers of the most elementary rights
to organize, let alone any broader political rights, by the exercise of
dictatorial managerial control in the factories as part of the
systematic subordination of consumption to production, and by the
existence of pervasive socio-economic inequalities (Cliff 1988: ch.
1). These features of Russian society made it impossible to describe
the USSR as a workers' state, however degenerated.

This argument established at most that the USSR was a class
society, in the Marxist sense of a society where the direct producers
were excluded from control of the productive forces by an
exploiting minority. But what kind of class society? The Johnson–
Forest tendency argued that the USSR was state-capitalist entirely
on the grounds of the existence of a 'hierarchy in the process of
production itself' (James 1986a: 37). This presumed, as James
(1986a: 31) argued, that 'the factory' was 'the centre of production
relations'. But this seemed to involve too narrow a conception of
capitalism. Marx (1973: 449) himself distinguished between the
analysis of 'capital in general, as distinct from the particular
capitals' and that of 'many capitals'. 'Capital in general' referred
above all to the immediate process of production analysed in
Capital Volume 1, where capitalist control of the labour process
makes possible the extraction of surplus-value from workers
compelled to sell their labour-power to secure their means of
existence. However, '[c]apital exists and can only exist as many
capitals' (Marx 1973: 414). The capitalist economy is necessarily
divided among competing firms. This process of competition is no
mere secondary feature of the capitalist mode of production. On the
contrary, '[t]he influence of individual capitals upon one another
has the effect precisely that they must conduct themselves as *capital*'
(Marx 1973: 657). Competition in particular compels capitals to
accumulate, to reinvest surplus-value in expanding output and
improving productivity. The accumulation process in turn underlies

the main tendencies of the capitalist mode, in particular, the centralization and concentration of capital and the trend for the rate of profit to fall underlying the theory of crises that is the centrepiece of *Capital* Volume 3. (The interpretation of *Capital* outlined above is most fully developed in the *chef d'oeuvre* of the Ukrainian Trotskyist Roman Rosdolsky (1977); see also Callinicos 1982a ch. 3.)

Marx's analysis of capitalism thus involves a theory of the relations among the exploiters as well as of those between exploiters and exploited. This consideration underlays the insistence by Trotsky and his orthodox followers as well as by Burnham, Shachtman and Castoriadis, that the complete statization of an economy would involve its liberation of the laws of motion of capitalism. A state-controlled economy was one in which the market had been suppressed, thereby removing the process of competition through which individual units of production are compelled 'to conduct themselves as *capital*'. Cliff's solution to this problem was simple. Considered in isolation from the rest of the world, the internal workings of the Soviet economy could be understood as if 'Russia were one big factory managed directly from one centre' (Cliff 1988: 221). The 'many capitals' had been eliminated within the USSR. But, of course Russia was in fact part of the international state system and subject to the competitive pressures at work within it. These pressures took the form mainly of the military rivalries between the USSR and Western capitalism – in the inter-war period, chiefly Britain and then Germany, after 1945 the USA and its allies – but their effects were the same as those deriving from the market. Military competition forced the Russian bureaucracy to give priority to heavy industry and the arms sector. This, Cliff argued, was a form of capital accumulation, in which consumption is subordinated to production. Hence the period of the First Five Year Plan (1928–32) marked the turning point from what Lenin had called a 'workers' state with bureaucratic deformations' to state capitalism. Committed to building the industrial base essential to meet the military challenge from the West,

> the bureaucracy, transformed into a personification of capital, for whom the accumulation of capital is the be-all and end-all here, must get rid of all remnants of workers' control, must substitute conviction in the labour process by coercion, must atomize the working class, must force all social-political life into a totalitarian mould.
>
> (Cliff 1988: 165)

The horrors of the 1930s reflected the extremely concentrated fashion in which the 'primitive accumulation of capital', which took two centuries in Britain, was packed into ten years in the USSR.

Cliff's analysis of Stalinism followed Trotsky's theory of permanent revolution in taking the capitalist world system as its basic frame of reference: 'when Russia is viewed within the international economy the basic features of capitalism can be discerned: "anarchy in the social division of labour and despotism in that of the workship are mutual conditions of each other . . ."' (Cliff 1988: 221–2). In treating the effects of global competition as a necessary condition of the existence of state capitalism in the USSR Cliff avoided the main defect of James's version of the theory. James located state capitalism entirely in 'the process of production itself'. He consequently had no means of explaining why the Soviet bureaucracy enforced 'despotism in . . . the workshop'. Capitalism was thus reduced to the clash of wills between workers and management within the factory. Castoriadis's theory of 'bureaucratic capitalism' thus drew out the voluntarism implicit in any analysis which, like James's, reduces capitalist relations of production to class conflict in the immediate production process (the German 'capital-logic' school is another example of this approach: see Callinicos 1982a: ch. 6). Cliff's theory, by contrast, was able to explain the subjection of the working class in the USSR in the dynamic of capital accumulation by setting the Stalinist regime in its global context, the international state system dominated by military competition.

Marx and Trotsky aside, what other filiations within Marxism could Cliff's theory claim? Anderson (1984a: 125) calls the social-democratic theorist Karl Kautsky 'the father of "state capitalism"'. In fact, Cliff's and Kautsky's theories have little in common apart from their use of the expression 'state capitalism'. Kautsky dubbed the Bolshevik regime state-capitalist from 1917 onwards, on the grounds that the October Revolution took place in a backward country unready for socialism and broke with parliamentary democracy (Salvadori 1979; chs VIII, IX). The reasons reflected more Kautsky's evolutionist theory of history and reformist political strategy than an elaborated analysis of the USSR. Cliff, by contrast, regarded the October Revolution as a socialist revolution and dated the bureaucratic counter-revolution to the late 1920s. His own theory bore a kinship to, and was to some degree influenced by

Bukharin's writings during and immediately after the First World War. As early as 1915, Bukharin (1982: 17) argued that the tendencies towards the concentration and centralization of capital whose culmination Hilferding described as 'finance capital', the merger of banking and industrial capital, involved a trend for the state and private capital themselves to fuse, in turn involving 'the conversion of each developed "national system" of capitalism into a "state capitalist trust"'. At the same, 'the centre of gravity in the competitive struggle is carried over into the world market , whereas within the country competition dies out' (Bukharin 1982: 18). The form of competition thereby tended to change, as the rivalries of private firms in the market were subordinated to the military struggle between state capitals, a process culminating in the First World War. From this perspective, the Stalinist industrialization of the Soviet Union could be seen, not as the economic consolidation of a workers' state, but as an extreme form of a generalized tendency towards militarized state capitalism accelerated by the Great Depression of the 1930s and leading again to the outbreak of war at the end of the decade (Harman 1984: ch. 2).

What were the political implications of the theory of state capitalism? Cliff (1948: 142) concluded his original version of the theory by predicting that '[t]he class struggle in Stalinist Russia *must inevitably* express itself in gigantic spontaneous explosions of millions' that would be the 'first chapter of the victorious proletarian revolution', a perspective which he defended in later years against those such as Deutscher who expected the bureaucracy to reform itself (for example, Cliff 1982: 118–34, 166–91). But what about the West? Anderson (1984a: 124) argues that describing the USSR as a 'class society' necessarily involves an accommodation with Western capitalism, since the latter possesses the 'democratic liberties' absent in the East and therefore seems to be 'the lesser – because non-totalitarian – evil'. Shachtman's final destiny as a Cold War Democrat revealed the political truth of theories of state capitalism as well as of bureaucratic collectivism: 'The logic of these interpretations . . . always ultimately tended (though with individual, less consistent exceptions) to shift their adherents to the Right' (Anderson 1984a: 125) Anderson's logic does not seem compelling. Trotsky had refused to make a difference in political regime the basis of supporting one group of capitalist powers against another. Even in June 1940, after the fall of France, he had rejected the argument that the existence of parliamentary democracy in Britain made it a lesser evil than German fascism, and had argued that the contradictions involved in the Nazis' attempt to rule the Continent by force would provoke revolutionary explosions (Trotsky 1973d: 296–9). The *Socialist Review* group took a similar approach during the Cold War, refusing to support either the Eastern or the Western bloc, and instead basing their hopes on working-class revolt from below, a stance summed up by the slogan 'Neither Washington nor Moscow but International Socialism'. Viewing the East–West conflict as an inter-imperialist struggle implied the revolutionary defeatism first developed by Lenin during the First World War rather than Shachtman's Stalinophobia.

More generally, Cliff's theory of state capitalism made it possible to reinstate the idea of socialism as the self-emancipation of the working class to the central importance given it by Marx. If not only the Soviet Union but also the Eastern European states, China, Vietnam and Cuba represented, not a deformed socialism, but a variant of capitalism, then there was no question of socialism being achieved without the self-activity of the working class. It was also possible to defend a fairly orthodox version of the revolutionary socialist tradition as it had been developed by figures such as Lenin, Luxemburg, and Trotsky. The voluntarist theories of state or bureaucratic capitalism advanced by James and Castoriadis tended to identify socialism with spontaneous shopfloor revolt and therefore to reject the theory of a vanguard party and the associated strategy and tactics developed by Lenin and Trotsky in particular. Cliff's version of the theory of state capitalism required no such break with the classical Marxist tradition, as is indicated by his major study of Lenin (Cliff 1975–9), although the implied commitment to the construction of a revolutionary party was combined with a Luxemburgian stress on the essential and creative role played by spontaneous explosions of working-class revolt.

5.2 A progressive problem-shift?

'*A given fact is explained scientifically only if a new fact is explained with it*', Lakatos wrote. A research programme which predicts novel facts and at least some of whose predictions are corroborated is a 'progressive problem-shift' in the history of the sciences (Lakatos 1978: I, 33–4). Orthodox Trotskyism, by contrast, represented a 'degenerating problem-shift' since, as we saw in Chapters 2 and 3 above, it sought to rescue Trotsky's analysis of Stalinism from refutation by a series of defensive manoeuvres that lagged behind rather than anticipating the facts. How well does the variant of Trotskyism developed by Cliff stand up to an application of the same criteria? To answer this question requires first taking account of Elie Zahar's clarification of the nature of the novel facts which Lakatos requires a progressive programme to predict. On the basis of a discussion of Einstein's transformation of modern physics, Zahar argues that a novel fact need not be one unknown at the time of the predicting theory's formulation. Rather: '*A fact will be considered novel with respect to a given hypothesis if it did not belong to the problem-situation that governed the construction of the hypothesis*' (Zahar 1973: 103). Thus, if a theory formulated to resolve a specific scientific problem entails as a corollary some established fact not involved in that problem, it has successfully predicted a novel fact.

These considerations are relevant to the plight of post-war Trotskyism. For the FI was confronted, not simply with the triumph of Stalinism in the East, but with the expansion of capitalism in the West. Cliff (1987: 15), viewing post-war Britain from the perspective of colonial Palestine, was struck by the fact that

> [t]he standard of living for workers was high. When I first visited a worker's house – just an ordinary house – I asked his job and he was an engineer. My English wasn't very good so I thought he meant an engineer with a degree. But he was a semi-skilled engineering worker. It was a complete shock. Children were better off than in the thirties. The only time I saw children without shoes in Europe was in Dublin. Children didn't get rickets any more. This helped me to realize that the final crisis wasn't around the corner.

Cliff's first major contribution to the British Trotskyist movement was a critique, written in 1947, of Mandel's attempts to deny the existence of a post-war economic recovery (Cliff 1982: 24–37). Nevertheless, the fact that 'the final crisis wasn't around the corner' played no part in the 'problem-situation' involved in the formulation of Cliff's theory of state capitalism. That, rather, was defined by what Cliff (1948: i) regarded as the 'unbridgeable antagonism between the definition of Russia as a degenerated workers' state and fundamental elements of Marxism such as . . .

the self-mobilization and self-conscious action of the masses as a necessary element for the socialist revolution'.

Implicit, however, in Cliff's analysis of state capitalism was an explanation of the post-war boom. This analysis identified military competition between East and West as the chief mechanism enforcing the dynamic of capital accumulation on the USSR. The escalation of the Cold War led to unprecedentedly high levels of peacetime arms expenditure, particularly in the two superpowers. In 1962 military spending corresponded to half of world gross capital formation (Kidron 1970: 49). Now arms production has, from the standpoint of Marxist economic theory, peculiar properties. It neither provides new means of production (Department I) nor contributes to the consumption of the working class (Department IIa). The output of the arms sector therefore does not feed back, either directly or indirectly, into further production. It is a form of unproductive consumption, analogous to the consumption of luxuries by the capitalists themselves (Department IIb or III) – Cliff (1948: 121–2) calls arms 'the collective consumption of the capitalist class', which enables that class through military expansion, 'to get new capital, new possibilities of accumulation'. It can be shown that, because arms, unlike capital or wage goods, do not re-enter the cycle of production, the rate of profit in the arms sector does not contribute to the formation of the general rate of profit. This has the very important corollary that, other things being equal, arms production has a stabilizing effect on the capitalist economy, for the following reasons: first, the diversion of surplus-value to military investments tends to slow down the rate of accumulation, and therefore the trend for the organic composition (the ratio of capital invested in means of production to capital invested in labour-power) to rise thereby, since, according to Marx, only labour creates profits, bringing down the general rate of profit; second, a higher than average organic composition of capital in the arms sector will not cause a rise in the general rate of profit; and third, arms production, by employing unused factors, will stimulate demand, with the consequences for output and employment that Keynesian economics would lead us to expect (see Harman 1984: 35–46).

Cliff drew on some of these stabilizing properties of arms production to help explain why Russian state capitalism did not experience the classical cycle of boom and slump characteristic of market economies (Cliff 1948: 121–25, much truncated in later versions; compare Cliff 1988: 243–4). Only later did he see that these properties could also help explain the long boom. His own version of this explanation, published in 1957, relied mainly on the third factor referred to above: the high levels of post-war arms production had secured full employment through their effect in stimulating demand (Cliff 1982: 101–7). It was Michael Kidron (1970; 1974; 1989), Cliff's closest collaborator in the 1950s and early 1960s, who developed a much more elaborated theory of the 'permanent arms economy', which, in this respect more faithful to Cliff's original discussion of military expenditure, focused on the role of arms production in offsetting the tendency of the rate of profit to fall. The most rigorous formulation of the theory was, however, provided much later by Chris Harman (1984). The theory of the permanent arms economy allowed the International Socialists to acknowledge the reality of the boom of the 1950s and 1960s and to avoid the kinds of response characteristic of orthodox Trotskyism – the catastrophic fantasies of Healy and the apologetic manoeuvres of Mandel. At the same time, however, the theory predicted that capitalism was experiencing an only temporary stabilization. Cliff (1948: 121–5) had pointed out that arms expenditure, by diverting surplus-value from productive investment, tended to prevent slumps at the price of a long-term tendency toward stagnation. Those economies with a relatively high level of arms expenditure, finding themselves at a competitive disadvantage, would react by increasing the share of investment taken by civilian industries, and thereby allow the tendencies towards a classical business cycle to reassert themselves (see, for example, Cliff 1982: 106–7). On this analysis, then, the growing rivalries within the Western bloc between the USA, on the one hand, and Japan and West Germany, on the other, were a foreseeable consequence of the uneven distribution of the arms burden within the Atlantic alliance whose outcome, lower American military spending, could only lead to a decline in the rate of profit and global recessions such as those of 1974–5 and 1979–82 (see Harman 1984: 93–9).

Cliff's theory of state capitalism, and its extension in the theory of the permanent arms economy, had two further consequences. First, they provided a basis for understanding developments in the Third World. Kidron (1974: ch. 6) and Nigel Harris (1971) challenged certain elements of Lenin's theory of imperialism, and in particular the idea that the colonies (by then increasingly ex-colonies) played an essential role for the advanced countries as markets, sources of raw materials, and investment sites, Harris attempted to show in some detail that, as a result of the drive to autarky by the major powers in the 1930s, and of the post-war arms economy, the major flows of trade and investment in the world market took place among the advanced countries themselves. The Third World was, on the whole, of *declining* economic significance to the Western metropolis. This shift in the global centre of economic gravity had made possible the relatively peaceful dismantlement of the European colonial empires after 1945; it also suggested a bleak future for the newly independent states, pursuing economic development while denied access to the productive resources concentrated in the West. Kidron and Harris sometimes drew the extreme conclusion that *any* development in the Third World was impossible, a claim refuted by the rise of the newly industrializing countries (see Harris 1986 and Callinicos 1987b). Nevertheless, their modification of Lenin's theory of imperialism allowed them to challenge the belief, very influential on the Western Left from the 1950s onwards, that national liberation movements in the Third World represented the main challenge to capitalism. Cliff (1982: 108–17) provided a critique of Lenin's theory of the labour aristocracy, often used to justify this belief on the grounds that the Western working class had been politically incorporated by receiving a share of the fruits of colonial exploitation. The main division in the world, Cliff and Kidron affirmed, was that between international capital and international labour, irrespective of the national sites of their struggle. For socialists in the West, therefore, '[t]he best service we can render international socialism is to help stoke up the fires at home' (Kidron 1974: 164).

But how did the great Third World revolutions – China, Vietnam, Cuba – fit into this analysis? Orthodox Trotskyists saw them as a confirmation of Trotsky's theory of permanent revolution and argued that they had resulted in new but deformed workers' states (see Section 3.2 above). Cliff rejected this conclusion, since it implied that socialism could be achieved without the self-activity of the working class. The theory of permanent revolution had assumed that the colonial bourgeoisie, dependent on foreign capital and fearful of its own working class, would not lead the struggle against imperialism and that therefore the proletariat would take on the tasks of both the bourgeois-democratic and the proletarian revolutions (see Section 1.1 above). But what would happen if the working class also did not lead the movement for national liberation? Cliff adduced various factors – above all, the political subordination of the working class in the backward countries, its domination by the politics of class collaboration, usually through the agency of Stalinism – to account for the proletariat's passivity in the Third World. The resulting vacuum was filled by another social force, the urban intelligentsia, radicalized by the deprivations and humiliations of colonial rule, inspired by Stalinist Russia's apparent success in industrializing on the basis of national autarky. National liberation movements, led by such intellectuals and usually marching under the banner of 'Marxism-Leninism', waged peasant wars which were able, in favourable conditions, to break the foreign hold on their countries. The new revolutionary regimes were not, however, workers' states of any description, but rather new bureaucratic state capitalisms reproducing the original Stalinist pattern. Cliff (1983) described this process as 'deflected permanent revolution': the social dynamics analysed by Trotsky, in the absence of working-class movements led by Marxist parties, led to a peculiar variant of bourgeois revolution.

What, secondly, were the implications of the analysis of contemporary capitalism developed by Cliff and his collaborators for the Western working class? One main effect of the long boom was, they argued, 'a shift in the locus of reformism' (see, for example, Cliff and Barker 1966; Barker 1973; Cliff 1982: 218–38). Full employment allowed workers to achieve significant improvements in their standard of living through small-scale wage disputes in individual plants or even sections. Consequently, the social-democratic and Communist parties, oriented on parliamentary reform, became less important to rank-and-file workers. The latter's most intense loyalties were attached instead to informal workplace institutions such as the British shop stewards, directly responsive to trade unionists' pressures and effective instruments of the guerilla warfare in the factories which pushed up wages independently of national bargaining. The political apathy of the 'affluent worker', documented and lamented by many scholars and commentators at the turn of the 1950s, represented not the end of the class struggle but its diversion into different channels. The increasing difficulties experienced by the world economy in the second half of the 1960s, however, meant that the ruling class would be compelled to curtail this 'do-it-yourself reformism' on the shopfloor – for example, through the imposition of wage controls. The resulting confrontation between capitalist offensive and a militant, self-confident rank and file would be explosive, particularly because of the decay of the mass reformist organizations:

> The concept of apathy or privatization is not a static concept. At a stage of development – when the path of individual reforms is being narrowed or closed – apathy can transform into its opposite, swift mass action. However, this new turn comes as an outgrowth of the previous stage; the epilogue and the prologue combine. Workers who have lost their loyalty to the traditional organizations, which have shown themselves to be paralysed over the years, are forced into extreme, explosive struggles on their own.
>
> (Cliff 1982: 234)

5.3 The experience of defeat

Britain in the late 1960s and the early 1970s seemed amply to bear out this perspective. The incomes policies imposed by first Labour and then Conservative governments led to the transformation of decentralized pay militancy into national strikes which increasingly took the form of confrontations between the trade-union movement and the state. In 1972 a miners' strike run from below by rank-and-file activists led to the Heath government's humiliating defeat, and was closely followed by dockers' successful defiance of the Industrial Relations Act; a second miners' strike at the beginning of 1974 brought the government down. In this climate of highly politicized industrial disputes, the International Socialists swelled by students radicalized by the *annus mirabilis* of 1968, grew rapidly, reaching at the time of Heath's fall a membership of over 3,000, many of them shop stewards in militant factories. Their experience was by no means unique. The years 1968–76 saw the biggest upturn in class struggle Western Europe had experienced since the immediate aftermath of the Russian Revolution – the French general strike of May–June 1968, the Italian 'hot autumn' of 1969, the Portuguese Revolution of 1974–5, the strikes which contributed to the death agony of the Franco regime in Spain. The European far Left was able in these circumstances to increase in size and establish a small but respectable working-class base. The greatest beneficiary was Maoism, the chief influence in Italy, for example, where the three main far left organizations at their height had 30,000 members between them and each produced a daily paper. Nevertheless, Trotskyist groups also experienced comparable growth – the International Socialists in Britain and the USFI sections in France and Spain, for example. (For a general account of the upturn of the late 1960s and its political consequences, see Harman 1988.)

Nothing was more natural than for the far Left to assume a continuation of this process, in which escalating workers' struggles would make possible the construction of mass revolutionary parties capable of challenging the social-democratic and Communist parties for the leadership of the Western labour movement. Even the fairly detached *trotskysant* Perry Anderson (1976: 101) could write in 1974 that the 'preliminary signs' of the 'reunification of theory and practice in a mass revolutionary movement, free of bureaucratic trammels', were 'visible'. Such expectations were dashed in the second half of the 1970s. Instead of a progressive radicalization of the workers' movement, new or revived social-democratic parties were able to establish themselves as the dominant force on the Left, containing working-class militancy and redirecting it towards electoral politics – a process which led to the victories of François Mitterrand in France, Felipe González in Spain, and Andreas Papandreou in Greece (Birchall 1986). In Britain the 1974–9 Labour government was able, thanks to the Social Contract it negotiated with the leaders of the Trade Union Congress, to defuse the shop-floor militancy which had broken the Heath government. The International Socialists' analysis of the decay of the mass reformist organizations had, while accurately capturing the latter's erosion as the institutional framework of working-class life, underestimated the residual political loyalty of even militant trade unionists towards the Labour Party, which could play a crucial role in circumstances of economic and political turmoil. Looking back on the early 1970s Cliff (1987: 19) commented:

> We understood the [political] generalization in terms of what workers didn't want. They didn't want incomes policy; they didn't want the Industrial Relations Act; they didn't want the Tories. But we weren't at all clear what workers wanted in a positive sense. When they shouted 'Heath out' we didn't understand that they wanted

Labour in. So we weren't clear what the impact of a Labour government would be.

The revival of the traditional reformist parties in the second half of the 1970s was followed by the introduction of neo-liberal economic policies which, whether implemented by the Thatcher government in Britain or the Mitterrand administration in France, undermined many post-war reforms. This increasingly unfavourable political climate, combined with the disappointment of their earlier hopes, threw the European far Left into profound crisis (Harman 1979; 1988: ch. 16). The Maoist organizations were worst affected, both because of the usually fairly crude Stalinist basis of their theory, and under the impact of the extraordinary reversals of Chinese politics after Mao's death, but the Trotskyist groups also suffered. The Ligue Communiste Révolutionnaire, the French section of the USFI, lost one of its most talented leaders, Henri Weber, to the Socialist Party (see Weber 1988), and suffered a serious decline in its membership, cohesion and influence. The British International Socialists (SWP from 1977 on) went through an acute crisis at the end of the 1970s, in which the main issues were, first the very question of whether or not the upturn which had brought down Heath was over, and second, the problem of how to relate the 'new social movements' responding to various forms of oppression (of women, blacks, gays, etc.) to the working-class struggle for socialism. Eventually these arguments were resolved and the SWP was able to weather ten years of Thatcherism with a membership of something over 4,000 in good political spirits. Some other Trotskyist groups also did not decline – for example, Lutte Ouvrière in France, the only organization of any significance to have stuck to the FI's original position after 1945, according to which the USSR was a workers' state and the Eastern European states bourgeois, an analysis so flagrantly inconsistent that Lutte Ouvrière cultivated a disdain for theoretical discussion and pragmatically concentrated instead on building up groups of its factory supporters.

Those Trotskyist organizations, such as the British SWP and Lutte Ouvrière, which emerged from the 1980s in reasonable shape found themselves in a considerably more difficult environment than that of the late 1960s and early 1970s. The Western labour movement remained fairly quiescent, in part thanks to the long recovery which most advanced economies enjoyed from the recession of the early 1980s. Usually fairly right-wing versions of social democracy were politically dominant on the Left. The intellectual climate was characterized by the most strenuous rejection of Marxism seen since the days of the liberal anti-Communism at the beginning of the Cold War – a rejection which often took the form of a supposedly more radical 'post-Marxism' or even 'post-modernism'. The Trotskyists' response was to argue that the 1980s were only an interlude, a temporary stabilization of Western capitalism whose foundations were far more fragile than those of the long boom of the 1950s and 1960s, and that further economic crises and social explosions lay ahead (see, for example, Krivine and Bensaid 1988; Harman 1988; Callinicos 1990). They could also say something else.

The socialist movement has been engaged, certainly since the turn of the nineteenth century and arguably since Blanqui challenged the gradualism of the Utopian socialists in the France of Louis Philippe, in a debate between the advocates of reform and revolution, between those who believe that it is possible peacefully to transform capitalism and those who argue that the working class will have forcibly to overthrow the bourgeois state. Eduard Bernstein and Rosa Luxemburg offered the classic statements of these two opposed cases, but it is an argument that has frequently recurred, for example in the controversy in the late 1950s provoked by Anthony Crosland's *The Future of Socialism*. Since the 1930s it has been Trotskyism that has provided the most consistent statements of the revolutionary case, for two reasons. First, Trotsky's writings on strategy and tactics extended and generalized the arguments of earlier revolutionary socialists such as Marx, Lenin and Luxemburg. Second, the emergence of regimes that claim to be socialist but which are domestically oppressive and internationally conservative required the formulation of a variant of Marxism that offered both an analysis of these regimes and a strategy for their overthrow – revolutionary socialism could be maintained only by its extension to the critique of Stalinism as well as that of capitalism; once again, Trotsky initiated this critique. The political and intellectual heritage he left his followers was, as we have seen, by no means unproblematic. This book has been devoted to exploring the different resolutions of the dilemmas of this heritage made by the three main variants of Trotskyism. As with the alternative endings of John Fowles's novel *The French Lieutenant's Woman*, my own view of which represents the most adequate response is indicated by my choice of which to place last. But however that may be, the fact ⚑ remains that as long as the dialogue between reform and revolution continues, Trotskyism will claim its own place as the continuation of the classical Marxist tradition with its orientation on working-class self-emancipation from below. It would be a rash social theorist who declared the great debate over the transformation of capitalism over.

Bibliography

Ali, T., (ed.) (1984). *The Stalinist Legacy*. Harmondsworth, Penguin.

Ali, T. (1987). *Street Fighting Years*. London, Collins.

Ali, T. (1988). *Revolution from Above*. London, Hutchinson.

Anderson, P. (1966). Socialism and pseudo-empiricism. *New Left Review*, 35, 2–42.

Anderson, P. (1974a). *Passages from Antiquity to Feudalism*. London, New Left Books.

Anderson, P. (1974b). *Lineages of the Absolutist State*. London, New Left Books.

Anderson, P. (1976). *Considerations on Western Marxism*. London, New Left Books.

Anderson, P. (1976–7). The antinomies of Antonio Gramsci. *New Left Review*, 100, 5–78.

Anderson, P. (1980). *Arguments within English Marxism*. London, Verso.

Anderson, P. (1984a). Trotsky's interpretation of Stalinism. In T. Ali (ed.), *The Stalinist Legacy*. Harmondsworth, Penguin, 118–28.

Anderson, P. 1984b. Preface. In I. Deutscher, *Marxism, Wars and Revolutions*. London, Verso, i–xx.

Bahro, R. (1978). *The Alternative in Eastern Europe*. London, New Left Books.

Bambery, C. (1987). The politics of James P. Cannon. *International Socialism*, 36, 49–89.

Bambery, C. (1989). Not all in it together. *Socialist Worker Review*, 123, 18–21.

Barker, C. (1973). The British Labour Movement. *International Socialism*, 61, 40–8.

Barnes, J. (1980). Marxism and the class struggle today. In M.–A. Waters *et al.*, *Proletarian Leadership in Power*. New York, Socialist Workers' Party, 16–31.

Barnes, J. (1983). Their Trotsky and ours. *New International* (New York), 1:1, 9–89.

Beilharz, P. (1987). *Trotsky, Trotskyism and the Transition to Socialism*. Beckenham, Croom Helm.

Bensaid, D. (1988). The formative years of the Fourth International (1933–1938). *Notebooks for Study and Research* (Paris), 9, 3–47.

Binns, P. and Haynes, M. (1980). New theories of Eastern European class societies. *International Socialism*, 2:7, 18–50.

Birchall, I. (1980). The autonomy of theory. *International Socialism*, 2:10, 51–91.

Birchall, I. (1986). *Bailing Out the System*. London, Bookmarks.

Bornstein, S. and Richardson, A. (1986a). *Against the Stream*. London, Socialist Platform.

Bornstein, S. and Richardson. (1986b). *War and the International*. London, Socialist Platform.

Bloom, A. (1986). *Prodigal Sons*. New York, Oxford University Press.

Buhle, P. (ed.) (1986). *C. L. R. James*. London, Allison and Busby.

Buhle, P. (1988). *C. L. R. James*. London, Verso.

Bukharin, N. I. (1982). *Selected Writings on the State and the Transition to Socialism*. Nottingham, Spokesman.

Burnham, J. (1940). Letter of resignation from the Workers Party. *Fourth International* (New York), 1:4, 106–7.

Burnham, J. (1962). *The Managerial Revolution*. Harmondsworth, Penguin.

Burnham, J. and Shachtman, M. (1939). Intellectuals in Retreat. *New International* (New York), V:1, 3–22.

Callinicos, A. (1982a). *Is there a Future for Marxism?* London, Macmillan.

Callinicos, A. (1982b). Trotsky's theory of permanent revolution and its relevance to the Third World today. *International Socialism*, 2:16, 98–112.

Callinicos, A. (1983). *Marxism and Philosophy*. Oxford, Clarendon.

Callinicos, A. (1984). Their Trotskyism and ours. *International Socialism*, 2:22, 117–42.

Callinicos, A. (1987a). *Making History*. Cambridge, Polity.

Callinicos, A. (1987b). Imperialism, capitalism and the State today. *International Socialism*, 2:35, 71–115.

Callinicos, A. (1988). *South Africa between Reform and Revolution*. London, Bookmarks.

Callinicos, A. (1989). Bourgeois revolutions and historical materialism. *International Socialism*, London, 2:43, 113–71.

Callinicos, A. (1990). *Against Postmodernism*. Cambridge, Polity.

Cannon, J. P. (1970). *Socialism on Trial*. New York, Pathfinder.

Cannon, J. P. (1972). *The Struggle for a Proletarian Party*. New York, Pathfinder.

Cannon, J. P. (1973a). *Speeches to the Party*. New York, Pathfinder.

Cannon, J. P. (1973b). *Notebook of an Agitator*. New York, Pathfinder.

Cannon, J. P. (1977). _The Struggle for Socialism in the 'American Century'._ New York, Pathfinder.

Castoriadis, C. (1987). _The Imaginary Institution of Society._ Cambridge, Polity.

Castoriadis, C. (1988a) _Political and Social Writings_, 2 vols. Minneapolis, University of Minnesota Press.

Catoriadis, C. (1988b). The Gorbachev interlude. _New Politics_ (New York), 1:4 (NS), 60–79.

Ciliga, A. (1979). _The Russian Enigma._ London, Ink Links.

Claudin, F. (1975). _The Communist Movement._ Harmondsworth, Penguin.

Cliff, T, (1948). The Nature of Stalinist Russia. _RCP Internal Bulletin_, 1–142.

Cliff, T. (1975–9). _Lenin_, 4 vols. London, Pluto.

Cliff. T. (1982). _Neither Washington nor Moscow._ London, Bookmarks.

Cliff, T. (1983). _Deflected Permanent Revolution._ London, Bookmarks.

Cliff, T. (1987). Fifty-five years a revolutionary. _Socialist Worker Review_, 100, 14–19.

Cliff, T. (1988). _State Capitalism in Russia._ London, Bookmarks.

Cliff, T. (1989). _Trotsky_, 1: _Towards October._ London, Bookmarks.

Cliff, T., _et al._ (1971). _The Fourth International, Stalinism and the Origins of the International Socialists._ London, Pluto.

Cliff, T., and Barker, C. (1966). _Incomes Policy, Legislation and Shop Stewards._ London, International Socialism.

Curtis, D. A. (1988). Foreword. In C. Castoriadis, _Political and Social Writings._ Minneapolis, University of Minnesota Press, I, vii–xxiii.

Davis, M. (1986). _Prisoners of the American Dream._ London, Verso.

Deutscher, I (1949). _Stalin._ Oxford, Oxford University Press.

Deutscher, I. (1967). _The Unfinished Revolution._ Oxford, Oxford University Press.

Deutscher, I. (1970a) _The Prophet Armed._ Oxford, Oxford University Press.

Deutscher, I. (1970b). _The Prophet Unarmed._ Oxford, Oxford University Press.

Deutscher, I. (1970c). _The Prophet Outcast._ Oxford, Oxford University Press.

Deutscher, I. (1984). _Marxism, Wars and Revolutions._ London, Verso.

Dobbs, F. (1972). _Teamster Rebellion._ New York, Pathfinder.

Draper, H. (1977). _Karl Marx's Theory of Revolution_, Vol. I. New York, Monthly Review.

Ervin, C. W. (1988–9). Trotskyism in India, I. _Revolutionary History_, 1:4, 22–34.

Filtzer, D. (1986). _Soviet Workers and Stalinist Industrialization._ London, Pluto.

Fisk, M. (1977). *Socialism from Below in the United States*. Cleveland, Hera.

Fourth International (1948). The USSR and Stalinism. *Fourth International* (New York), 9:4, 110–28.

Fourth International (1969a). The class nature of Eastern Europe. In *Class, Party, and State and the Eastern European Revolution*. New York, Socialist Workers' Party, 53–5.

Fourth International (1969b). The Yugoslav Revolution. In *Class, Party, and State and the Eastern European Revolution*. New York, Socialist Workers' Party, 56–61.

Frank, E. R. (1944). The European Revolution – its Prospects and Tasks. *Fourth International* (New York), 5:12, 378–82.

Frank, P. (1969). The evolution of Eastern Europe. In *Class, Party and State and the Eastern European Revolution,* New York, Socialist Workers' Party, 47–53.

Frank, P. (1979). *The Fourth International*. London, Ink Links.

Georgakas, D. (1986). Young Detroit radicals, 1955–1965. In P. Buhle (ed.), *C. L. R. James*. London, Allison and Busby, 185–94.

Germain, E. (1946). The first phase of the European Revolution. *Fourth International* (New York), 7:8, 230–5.

Germain, E. (1974). What should be modified and what should be maintained in the theses of the Second World Congress of the Fourth International on the question of Stalinism? In *International Secretariat Documents*. New York, Socialist Workers' Party, I, 16–24.

Giddens, A. (1981). *A Contemporary Critique of Historical Materialism*. London, Macmillan.

Gramsci, A. (1971). *Selections from the Prison Notebooks*. London, Lawrence and Wishart.

Gramsci, A. (1977). *Selections from the Political Writings 1910–1920*. London, Lawrence and Wishart.

Grant, T. (1989). *The Unbroken Thread*. London, Fortress Books.

Groves, R. (1974). *The Balham Group*. London, Pluto.

Habermas, J. (1987). *The Philosophical Discourse of Modernity*. Cambridge, Polity.

Hallas, D. (1969). Building the Leadership. *International Socialism*, 40, 25–32.

Hallas, D. (1971). The Stalinist parties. In T. Cliff *et al., The Fourth International, Stalinism and the Origins of the International Socialists*. London, Pluto, 65–75.

Hallas, D. (1972). Against the stream. *International Socialism*, 53, 30–39.

Hallas, D. (1973). Fourth International in decline. *International Socialism*, 60, 17–23.

Hallas, D. (1979). *Trotsky's Marxism*. London, Pluto.

Hallas, D. (1985). *The Comintern*. London, Bookmarks.

Hallas, D. (1988). Trotsky's heritage. *International Socialism*, 40, 53–64.

Halliday, F. (1983). *The Making of the Second Cold War*. London, Verso.

Hansen, J. (1969), The problem of Eastern Europe. In *Class, Party, and State and the Eastern European Revolution*, New York, Socialist Workers' Party, 20–35.

Harman, C. (1978). Mandel's *Late Capitalism. International Socialism*, 2:1, 79–96.

Harman, C. (1979). The crisis of the European revolutionary Left. *International Socialism*, 2:4, 49–87.

Harman, C. (1983). *Class Struggles in Eastern Europe, 1945–83*. London, Pluto.

Harman, C. (1984). *Explaining the Crisis*. London, Bookmarks.

Harman, C. (1988). *The Fire Last Time*. London, Bookmarks.

Harris, N. (1971). Imperialism today. In N. Harris and J. Palmer (eds), *World Crisis*. London, Hutchinson, 67–117.

Harris, N. (1986). *The End of the Third World*. London, I. B. Tauris.

Hill, C. (1984). *The Experience of Defeat*. London, Faber.

Hodgson, G. (1975). *Trotsky and Fatalistic Marxism*. Nottingham, Spokesman.

Howe, I. (1982). *A Margin of Hope*. New York, Harcourt Brace Jovanovich.

IKD Committee Abroad (1943). The National Question – Three Theses. *Workers' International News*, 5:10, 9–11.

Jacoby, R. (1987). *The Last Intellectuals*. New York, Basic.

James, C. L. R. (1963). *The Black Jacobins*. New York, Vintage.

James, C. L. R. (1980). *Notes on Dialectics*. London, Allison and Busby.

James, C. L. R. (1983). Interview. in MARHO, *Visions of History*. Manchester, Manchester University Press, 265–77.

James, C. L. R. (1986a) *State Capitalism and World Revolution*. Chicago, Charles H. Kerr.

James, C. L. R. (1986b). Interview. In P. Buhle, ed., *C. L. R. James*. London, Allison and Busby, 164–7.

James, C. L. R. *et al.* (1974) *Facing Reality*. Detroit, Bewick.

James, C. L. R. and Glaberman, M. (1986). Letters. In P. Buhle (ed.), *C. L. R. James*. London, Allison and Busby, 153–63.

Kagarlitsky, B. (1988). *The Thinking Reed*. London, Verso.

Kidron, M. (1970). *Western Capitalism since the War*. Harmondsworth, Penguin.

Kidron, M. (1974). *Capitalism and Theory*. London, Pluto.

Kidron, M. (1989). *A Permanent Arms Economy*. London, Bookmarks.

Krivine, A. and Bensaid, D. (1988). *Mai Si!* Paris, La Brèche-PEC.

Lakatos, I. (1976). *Proofs and Refutations*. Cambridge, Cambridge University Press.

Lakatos, I. (1978). *Philosophical Papers*, 2 vols. Cambridge, Cambridge University Press.

Löwy, M. (1981). *The Politics of Combined and Uneven Development.* London, Verso.

McGregor, S. (1986). The history and politics of *Militant. International Socialism*, 2:33, 59–88.

MacIntyre, A. (1971). *Against the Self-images of the Age.* London, Duckworth.

MacIntyre, A. (1981). *After Virtue.* London, Duckworth.

MacIntyre, A, (1988). *Whose Justice? Which Rationality?* London, Duckworth.

MacIntyre, S. (1980). *A Proletarian Science.* Cambridge, Cambridge University Press.

Mandel, E. (1975) *Late Capitalism.* London, New Left Books.

Mandel, E. (1979a). *Trotsky.* London, New Left Books.

Mandel, E. (1979b). *Revolutionary Marxism Today.* London, New Left Books.

Mandel, E. (1983). In Defence of the Permanent Revolution. *International Viewpoint* (Paris), 32.

Mandel, E. (1986). *The Meaning of the Second World War.* London, Verso.

Marx, K. (1973). *Grundrisse.* Harmondsworth, Penguin.

Marx, K., and Engels, F. (1965). *Selected Correspondence.* Moscow, Progress.

Marx, K., and Engels, F, (1975). *Collected Works.* Vol. 3: *Marx and Engels 1843–44.* London, Lawrence and Wishart.

Marx, K., and Engels F. (1976a). *Collected Works, Vol. 5: Marx and Engels 1845–47.* London, Lawrence and Wishart.

Marx, K., and Engels, F. (1976b). *Collected Works.* Vol. 6: *Marx and Engels 1845–48.* London, Lawrence and Wishart.

Molyneux, J. (1981). *Leon Trotsky's Theory of Revolution.* Brighton, Harvester.

Morrow, F. (1943). Our differences with the three theses. *Workers' International News*, 5:10, 11–12.

Morrow, F. (1944). The first phase of the European Revolution. *Fourth International* (New York), 5:12, 368–77.

Pablo, M. (1974a). Where are we going? In *International Secretariat Documents.* New York, Socialist Workers' Party, I, 4–12.

Pablo, M. (1974b). The building of the Revolutionary Party. In *International Secretariat Documents.* New York, Socialist Workers' Party, I, 30–40.

Popper, K. R. (1969). *Conjectures and Refutations.* London, Routledge and Kegan Paul.

Popper, K. R. (1970). *The Logic of Scientific Discovery.* London, Hutchinson.

Prager, R, (1988). The Fourth International during the Second World War. *Revolutionary History*, 1:3, 19–36.

Reiman, M. (1987). *The Birth of Stalinism*. London, I. B. Tauris.

Reisner, W., (ed.) (1973). *Documents of the Fourth International: The Formative Years (1933–40)*. New York, Pathfinder.

Rizzi, B. (1985). The Bureaucratization of the World. London, Tavistock.

Rosdolsky, R. (1977). *The Making of Marx's 'Capital'*, London, Pluto.

Rousset, P. (1975). *Le Parti communiste vietnamien*. Paris, Maspéro.

Sader, E. (1987). The Workers' Party in Brazil. *New Left Review*, 165, 93–102.

Salvadori, M. (1979). *Karl Kautsky and the Socialist Revolution 1880–1938*. London, New Left Books.

Segal, R. (1979). *The Tragedy of Leon Trotsky*, London, Hutchinson.

Shachtman, M. (1940). The crisis in the American Party. *New International* (New York), VI:2, 43–51.

Shachtman, M. (1962). *The Bureaucratic Revolution*. New York, Donald Press.

Solzhenitsyn, A. I. (1976). *The Gulag Archipelago*, II. London, Collins/Fontana.

Taaffe, P. (1986). *What We Stand For*. Militant, London.

Trotsky, L. (n.d.). *Our Political Tasks*. London, New Park.

Trotsky, L. (1963). *Diary in Exile 1935*. New York, Atheneum.

Trotsky, L. (1967). *The History of the Russian Revolution*, 3 vols. London, Sphere.

Trotsky, L. (1969). *Permanent Revolution and Results and Prospects*, New York, Pathfinder.

Trotsky, L. (1970). *The Revolution Betrayed*. New York, Pathfinder.

Trotsky, L. (1971a). *The Struggle against Fascism in Germany*. New York, Pathfinder.

Trotsky, L. (1971b). *Writings 1934–35*. New York, Pathfinder.

Trotsky, L. (1972a). *The First Five Years of the Communist International*, 2 vols. New York, Monad.

Trotsky, L. (1972b). *Writings 1933–34*. New York, Pathfinder.

Trotsky, L. (1972c). *Black Nationalism and Self-Determination*. New York, Pathfinder.

Trotsky, L. (1973a). *1905*. Harmondsworth, Penguin.

Trotsky, L. (1973b). *Writings 1930-31*. New York, Pathfinder.

Trotsky, L. (1973c). *In Defence of Marxism*. New York, Pathfinder.

Trotsky, L. (1973d). *Writings 1939–40*. New York, Pathfinder.

Trotsky, L. (1973e). *The Spanish Revolution*. New York, Pathfinder.

Trotsky, L. (1974). *Writings 1938–39*. New York, Pathfinder.

Trotsky, L. (1975). *The Challenge of the Left Opposition (1923–5)*. New York, Pathfinder.

Trotsky, L. (1976a). *On China*. New York, Monad.

Trotsky, L. (1976b). *Writings 1937–38*. New York, Pathfinder.

Trotsky, L. (1977). *The Crisis in the French Section (1935–36)*. New York, Pathfinder.

Trotsky, L. (1981). *The Challenge of the Left Opposition (1928–9)*. New York, Pathfinder.

Trotsky, L. *et al.* (1973). *Their Morals and Ours*. New York, Pathfinder.

Unger, R. M. (1987). *Social Theory: Its Situation and its Task*. Cambridge, Cambridge University Press.

Wald, A. M. (1987). *The New York Intellectuals*. Chapell Hill, University of North Carolina Press.

Wang Fan-hsi (1980). *Chinese Revolutionary*. Oxford, Oxford University Press.

Weber, H. (1975). *Marxisme et conscience de classe*. Paris, Union Générale d' Editions.

Weber, H. (1988). *Vingt ans après*. Paris, Seuil.

Westoby, A. (1985). Introduction. In B. Rizzi, *The Bureaucratization of the World*, London, Tavistock, 1–33.

Widgery, D. (1976). *The Left in Britain*. Harmondsworth, Penguin.

Wolforth, T. (1971). *The Struggle for Marxism in the United States*. New York, Bulletin.

Wolforth, T. (1988a). Revolutionaries in the 1950s. *Against the Current* (Detroit), 14, 28–35).

Wolforth, T, (1988b). Socialist politics after Hungary '56. *Against the Current* (Detroit), 15, 39–44.

Wolforth, T. (1989). Reclaiming Our Traditions. *Against the Current* (Detroit), 19, 44–5.

Wright, E. O. (1983). Capitalism's Futures. *Socialist Review* (Oakland), 68, 77–126.

Zahar, E. (1973). Why did Einstein's programme supersede Lorentz's? *British Journal of the Philosophy of Science*, 24, 95–123, 223–62.

Index